ARMAGEDDON AHEAD

DR. ROY HARTHERN
INTERNATIONAL BIBLE TEACHER

Published by

LIFEBRIDGE
BOOKS
P.O. BOX 49428
CHARLOTTE, NC 28277

Printed in the United States of America.

DEDICATION

I am dedicating this book to my beloved wife, Pauline. She has been my partner in ministry since we were married in January 1951. When I needed someone to encourage me, she was always the eternal optimist. When I needed godly counsel, I could always depend on her wisdom. When I needed someone to pray for me, Pauline was my constant prayer warrior and a tower of spiritual strength. Someone asked me recently why Pauline and I had never had an argument in the many years of our marriage while he and his wife were having verbal battles constantly. "That's easy," I replied, "You should have married Pauline."

I would also like to express my appreciation to my son-in-law, evangelist Benny Hinn for encouraging me to write this book. Every time he would phone or visit our family he would always ask if I had started to write the Book of Revelation. His persistence helped to motivate me.

My three daughters, Suzanne, Leanne, and Elizabeth have also encouraged me to write a book on prophecy. They offered to give me the resources to help launch this project.

Finally I want to thank the Lord for giving me a great desire to study Bible prophecy.

CONTENTS

INTRODUCTION

I entered full time ministry in 1945 and I have preached more sermons from the Book of Revelation than from any other book in the Bible.

After a service it is not unusual for several people to approach me and say, *I read the Bible regularly, but I have never been able to understand the Book of Revelation. It is too deep. How can I interpret all those prophetic symbols? How can I possibly understand the meaning of the beast with the seven heads and ten horns?*

I agree that while much of the Book of Revelation is symbolic (there are 35 symbols in the book), it should be read with the understanding that every symbol has a literal meaning. Many times the context will explain the meaning of the symbol and at other times the meaning will be explained by other passages in the Bible. Prophecy is history recorded before it happens.

SOME DISTURBING QUESTIONS

Here are a few of the disturbing questions I have been asked in recent days:
- Are we marching rapidly towards Armageddon?
- What is the meaning of the 4 horsemen of the Apocalypse?
- When will the world come to an end?
- Is the Antichrist alive today?
- Why does the Middle East continue to be a powder keg?
- When will the world be forced to take 666 to survive financially?

- What is the Mark of the Beast?
- Is the second coming of Christ imminent?
- Will Iran wipe Israel off the map as they have
  threatened?

The answers to these and many more questions are found in this book, *Armageddon Ahead.*

People Are Interested in Bible Prophecy

Bible prophecy has always been of great interest to young and old. Many of the Old Testament prophets predicted the events of the end time; Jesus taught about the prophetic signs of the last days; all of the New Testament writers wrote about future prophecy and in the 15th century, the prominent scientist, Sir Isaac Newton predicted, *In the end of time, God will raise up men who will devote their efforts to study the prophetic scriptures and insist on their literal interpretation.*

Even unbelievers are aware that these are troubling days. The events prophesied by Jesus in Matthew 24 as signs of the end time have always been part of world history, but we have never had all of these predicted events happen at the same time until now.

My Fascination With Bible Prophecy

For as long as I can remember, I have always had a fascination with Bible prophecy. As a small boy, I would be bored when I listened to most sermons, but whenever my pastor or a visiting minister would preach on the Second Coming of Christ or other prophetic sermons I would be excited.

My wife reminded me recently that soon after we were married, we returned to England to preach. We were staying with Pauline's parents and I was studying Bible prophecy for so many hours that I missed a meal with the family. Pauline's mother teasingly hid my books and insisted that I eat my meals on time. I had to comply in order to retrieve my books and resume my studies!

SETTING DATES IS FOOLISH

The longer I live and the closer we get to the Second Coming of Christ, the more interesting and exciting the Book of Revelation becomes. There have always been extremists who have set dates for the Coming of Christ. According to my research in preparation to write *Armageddon Ahead*, I discovered that the Jehovah's Witnesses allegedly have falsely predicted that Jesus would come and the world would end at six different times—1914, 1918, 1920, 1925, 1941, and 1975.

Even the Pope was reported to have celebrated Mass exactly at midnight on the last day of 999 A.D. and then stood motionless with upraised hands as church bells sounded to welcome the Coming of Christ. Obviously, the Pope was embarrassed because Jesus did not arrive. The Bible states that while this age of grace will come to an end when Jesus returns, the world will never end (Ephesians 3:21).

JESUS DID NOT COME IN 1988 OR 1989

Some years ago, I was invited to appear on several Christian television and radio stations to answer questions that were phoned in by concerned listeners. Some people were actually frightened. The reason was that a so-called prophecy expert had written a book entitled, *88 Reasons Why Jesus Will Come In 1988*. He even predicted the exact date of His return. Obviously Jesus did not appear, but the writer profited financially from the sales of his book—and when Jesus did not come as he had predicted, he had the audacity to write a second book to explain why he had missed it by one year. Of course, Jesus did not return in 1989 either, and fortunately, no one has heard of the writer since then.

Jesus said that *No one knows the day or the hour when He will come* (Matthew 24:36). We can know the signs of His return, but if Jesus said no one can know the day or the hour, that should end all speculation. Obviously Jesus is coming soon and while no one knows *when* He will return, we know that He *will*. We should live like He could come today but plan like we have another 100 years to live.

As You Read You Are Blessed

You are blessed whenever you read any book of the Bible; but the Book of Revelation is the only one that promises the reader a special blessing: *"Blessed is he who reads and those who hear the words of this prophecy, and keep those things which are written in it; for the time is near"* (Revelation 1:3).

Prophecy and Modern Technology

Many of the prophecies predicted in the Book of Revelation could not have been fulfilled in past years. Today, however, science and modern technology are producing weapons of mass destruction and the leaders of some nations are so morally corrupt that they are willing to use these nuclear weapons— and according to the Book of Revelation, they will.

Will Iran Wipe Israel off the Map?

Iran has threatened to remove the nation of Israel from the map. According to Bible prophecy, Iran, ancient Persia, will be one of the nations to ally with Russia and attack Israel in the last days. This invasion will lead to the Battle of Armageddon (Ezekiel 38 and 39).

This unholy alliance between Russia, Iran, and other Middle Eastern nations has already begun. If God is God and if the Bible is true, Israel will survive. History records the attempts of many men who have tried to annihilate Israel.

In my boyhood days, Hitler killed 6,000,000 Jews, yet today, Israel is a sovereign nation.

PEACE AND PROSPERITY? OR DOOM AND GLOOM?

Some view the Book of Revelation as a prophecy of doom, gloom, and despair. While most of the chapters describe the worst time of tribulation the world will ever know, these seven years of tribulation are the labor pains to birth an eternity of world peace and prosperity. As you read the Book of Revelation, remember that it is the story of Jesus the King, who is coming to establish His eternal Kingdom on this earth. This gives us hope in a hopeless and helpless world.

AN EASY TO UNDERSTAND TEXTBOOK

I have tried to write a simple commentary on the Battle of Armageddon and the Book of Revelation in easy to understand language. It is a simplified student's textbook and I trust that even new converts will easily grasp the truth and the meaning of the Book of Revelation.

I have used the New King James Version and have written my comments after each verse or after several verses.

In spite of the fact that many people think the Book of Revelation is a difficult book to understand, I will attempt to make it as simple as possible. Please send me an email with your thoughts and let me know if you think I succeeded. Thanks in advance for your reply. My contact information is on the last page of this book.

– En agape,
Roy Harthern

AN OVERVIEW

The Battle of Armageddon will be the final battle fought in the Middle East and in the world before Jesus returns to earth.

- At this battle the devil will be bound for 1,000 years, the Antichrist and his religious representative, the False Prophet, will be destroyed and the armies of the Antichrist will be defeated.
- After King Jesus has utterly destroyed His enemies and the enemies of Israel, He will establish His worldwide Kingdom with Jerusalem as His capital.
- He will reign for 1,000 years and after He has judged the unsaved and cast the devil and his hosts into the Lake of Fire at the Great White Throne Judgment, He will rule on the earth forever.

No Peace in the Middle East

- In spite of the repeated attempts of world leaders to bring peace to Israel and the Middle East, there will be no peace until the Antichrist makes a seven year peace treaty with Israel.
- This will introduce the Antichrist to the world and start what Bible teachers call *the seven year tribulation*.
- After three and a half years the Antichrist will break the peace treaty and he will invade the land of Israel in a final attempt to annihilate the Jewish nation.
- This will lead to the Battle of Armageddon.

THE ISLAMIC MESSIAH

- Many radical and fanatical Islamic leaders believe that the Messiah cannot return until the world is bathed in blood. Therefore they are committed to launch a nuclear war to destroy the big Satan, America and the little Satan, Israel.
- This is their sole motivation and until this war is fought, they believe the Messiah cannot return.
- They are not interested in diplomacy, because diplomacy postpones or negates war and they believe that only an international nuclear conflict will bring the Messiah back to earth to save the world from total destruction.
- The Battle of Armageddon will be their attempt to destroy the little Satan, Israel, and if, (as I pray) America allies with Israel, the Battle of Armageddon will be their chance to destroy the big Satan, America as well.

A BATTLE BETWEEN NATIONS

- Initially, the Battle of Armageddon will be a battle between the nations of the world.
- On one side will be the nations who ally with the Antichrist against Israel and the opposing armies will be those nations who fight to defend the nation of Israel against the Antichrist and his international military alliance.
- When the Antichrist and his armies start winning the war against Israel and it becomes obvious that Israel and her allies are heading for final defeat and total destruction, the Jews will pray for their Messiah to come and deliver them from the military might of the Antichrist's armies.

THE CLASH OF TWO CONFLICTING KINGDOMS

- In response to the prayers of the Jews, Jesus will appear in the clouds over the Mount of Olives in Jerusalem.

- Satan will deceive the Antichrist into believing that if he declares war against the Lord Jesus Christ, he can actually win the battle.
- Foolishly, the Antichrist listens to the devil's lie and the Battle of Armageddon ceases to be a war between nations and becomes a clash between two conflicting kingdoms, the Kingdom of God versus the kingdom of Satan; the Kingdom of Light versus the kingdom of darkness.
- The bad news is that the Battle of Armageddon will be the bloodiest and the most destructive conflict of all times.
- The good news is that the Antichrist will lose the battle and the Lord Jesus Christ will win the biggest victory in world history.
- Then Christ will establish His worldwide Kingdom of peace and prosperity on the earth.
- The Bible declares that the Battle of Armageddon will be won decisively in one day (Zechariah 14).
- When Jesus returns and the Battle of Armageddon has been won, the prayer that Jesus taught us to pray will be answered, *Thy Kingdom come; Thy Will be done on earth as it is done in heaven* (Matthew 6:10).

ANTICHRIST'S TERROR AND GOD'S JUDGMENT

- During the first half of the seven year tribulation, Israel will be persecuted by a ten nation confederation which will be formed as a political, financial, and military alliance within the area of the former Roman Empire (Daniel 7).
- Israel will also be persecuted by Mystical Babylon which is a false religious system (Revelation 17).
- Israel's initial persecution will not be as intense as in the final three and a half years because they will be protected by the Antichrist's peace treaty.

- During the entire seven years an angry God will be pouring out the seven seals of judgment, the seven trumpets of judgment and the seven bowls of judgment on a Christ rejecting world.
- These judgments occur consecutively and they become more severe until the final judgment which climaxes with the Battle of Armageddon and the Second Coming of Christ.
- These events are recorded in chapters 6 to 19.
- During the final half of the tribulation the Antichrist's supreme goal will be to annihilate Israel completely.
- Man will never experience such extreme and indescribable tribulation in recorded history.

THE MILLENNIUM

- When Jesus returns to earth to win the Battle of Armageddon, the Antichrist, the False Prophet, and the nations under the Antichrist's control will be destroyed and the devil will be bound in the abyss for 1,000 years.
- During the 1,000 years Jesus will rule on the earth (chapter 20).
- The 1,000 year's reign is called the Millennium.
- The word Millennium is taken from two Latin words meaning *1,000 years*.
- Satan and the unsaved will be judged and cast into the Lake of Fire at the end of the Millennium.
- The final two chapters of the Book of Revelation give us a brief glimpse of future eternity.

FOUR DIFFERENT INTERPRETATIONS

Since John wrote the Book of Revelation, scholars have usually held four different views of interpretation. They are:

1. The Preterist View

- This perspective places the Book of Revelation in the past, especially during the time of the Roman Empire in the first century.
- People who believe in this view teach that all the symbolism in the Book of Revelation was John's attempt to encourage the early church in its struggle against the persecution of Imperial Rome.
- They state that John believed the early church would understand the symbols of the Book of Revelation but that the Roman world would not.
- I do not agree that the Book of Revelation applied only to the first century.

2. The Historical View

- This position teaches that the Book of Revelation is a panoramic overview of history, past, present and future.
- The Seventh Day Adventist Church promotes this view.
- One major problem with this is that scholars do not all agree which event of history fits into which chapter of the Book of Revelation.
- I also do not accept this view.
- Another problem is that the average reader can get very confused because writers make different symbols mean different historical events.
- Some Bible passages which should be taken literally they make symbolic.
- In my preparation to write this book, I researched many writings by different authors from the Historical View and the more I read the more I realized how many different interpretations there are and I have recorded my response following their statements.

LISTED BELOW ARE SOME CONFUSING VIEWS FROM THE HISTORICAL INTERPRETATION

Interpretation: One writer stated that the two witnesses are the *Jews and the Gentiles*. Another said that they are the *Jews and the Church*. Still another writer maintained they are the *Old and New Testaments*. Others said that the two witnesses are *Elijah and John the Baptist; Elijah and Enoch and Elijah and Moses*. ***Response:*** I believe the two witnesses are Elijah and Enoch.

Interpretation: *The Book of Revelation is a history of the church.* ***Response:*** Not so! While the Book of Revelation was written to the church and chapters 2 and 3 are 7 messages to the church; from chapter 6 to chapter 19 it records God's dealings with Israel and the Antichrist's kingdom. These chapters cover the future seven year tribulation which is called, Daniel's 70th week (Daniel 9:27) and the Time of Jacob's (Israel's) trouble (Jeremiah 30:7).

Interpretation: *The seven seals deal with seven periods in the history of the church.* ***Response:*** Not so! They are seven seals of judgment God pours out on the earth in the early days and months of the future seven year tribulation.

Interpretation: *The white horse rider symbolizes a period of peace in the early church.* ***Response:*** Not so! The white horse rider symbolizes the future Antichrist.

Interpretation: *The red horse rider with a sword symbolizes the division between church leaders in church history.* ***Response:*** It does not! It is a symbol of war in the first half of the future seven year tribulation.

Interpretation: *The black horse rider, symbolizing famine, means the dark clouds of ignorance and superstition that swept over the Christian world.* *Response:* No! A famine means a famine.

Interpretation: *An earthquake means the breaking up of society. Another writer says an earthquake means that the foundations of the church were shaken. Still another states that an earthquake means the conviction of the Holy Spirit.* *Response:* No! An earthquake means an earthquake. There are four such earthquakes during the seven year tribulation and they are literal.

Interpretation: *A mountain symbolizes a city.* *Response:* Who says so? Why can't a mountain mean a mountain?

Interpretation: *An island means an influential family.* *Response:* This is absurd! The writer did not identify the family.

Interpretation: *The sun turning to darkness means that Christ was rejected.* *Response:* No! It means that the sun turned to darkness.

Interpretation: *The sun is a symbol of the Gospel.* *Response:* No! The sun is the sun.

Interpretation: *The moon is a symbol of Christ.* *Response:* No! The moon is the moon.

Interpretation: *One writer states that the moon turning to blood means the overthrow of authority. Another writes that the moon turning to blood is symbolic of Jesus shedding His blood.* *Response:* No! It means what it says.

Interpretation: *A star falling from heaven means the downfall of religious leaders.* **Response:** No! A star means a star unless the context makes the star an angel.

Interpretation: *The heavens departing as a scroll means the destruction of organized Christianity.* **Response:** No! Jesus gave the same prophecies in Matthew 24. The sun is the sun; the moon is the moon; stars are stars; and heaven is heaven.

Interpretation: *Trees, plants, and grass symbolize people.* **Response:** No! Trees mean trees; plants mean plants; and grass means grass.

Interpretation: *The 144,000 are not Jewish witnesses, they are a small remnant of the true church.* **Response:** How strange! Revelation 7 states that the 144,000 are made up of 12,000 Jews from 12 tribes of Israel and the 12 tribes are named. They will minister in the first half of the coming seven year tribulation. In fact, *all* of the above events will happen during the first half of the future seven year tribulation.

Interpretation: *Hail, fire, and blood falling from heaven in chapter 8 represent a storm of heresies, a mixture of dreadful errors falling on the church.* **Response:** Not so! Hail, fire, and blood mean hail, fire, and blood. They will fall from heaven in the future seven year tribulation.

Interpretation: *The star falling from heaven in chapters 8 and 9 refers to the Pope. Another writer says that it was some prominent person who corrupted the church.* **Response:** The writers do not name which Pope or the name of the prominent person.

Interpretation: *The mountain falling in the sea and the sea turning to blood mean the leaders of the persecutions in the church.* **Response:** No! A mountain is a mountain and the sea turning to blood means the sea turning to blood. All of these judgments will take place in the future seven year tribulation.

Interpretation: Smoke out of the abyss refers to false doctrine. *Response:* No! Smoke out of the abyss means just that.

Interpretation: The darkening of the planet in chapter 8 refers to spiritual darkness. *Response:* Who says so?

Interpretation: The locusts of chapter 9 mean the spread of false religion. *Response:* There is nothing in the Book of Revelation to suggest this.

Interpretation: The drying up of the river Euphrates means the end of the Turkish Empire. *Response:* Not so! Just as the Red Sea was the Red Sea and the river Jordan was the river Jordan and the Sea of Galilee was the Sea of Galilee, the river Euphrates is a river that runs through Iraq and Syria.

Interpretation: Trees and grass symbolize true believers. *Response:* The writer did not say which believers are trees and which believers are grass. How absurd!

Interpretation: The 200,000,000 demonic creatures in the 6th trumpet judgment in chapter 9 are not literal but symbolize Asiatic hordes that invaded Europe and Israel in past centuries. *Response:* Not so! The trumpets did not blow in past history, they will blow in the future seven year tribulation.

Interpretation: The 6th trumpet means that the power of the Turkish Empire has finished. They killed in war and brought a poisonous and ruinous religion. *Response:* No! The trumpet judgments are all future and will occur during the first half of the seven year tribulation.

Interpretation: The seven bowls of judgment are not literal, but *the fourth bowl and the fifth bowl of judgment are literal.* **Response:** Who gives this writer the authority to make such a decision? If the fourth and fifth bowls are literal, why don't we make all seven bowls literal?

Interpretation: *The temple in chapter 11 symbolizes the state of the church.* **Response:** Not so! The church will be raptured three and a half years before chapter 11.

Interpretation: *1260 days means 1260 years.* **Response:** Who says so?

Interpretation: *The sun clad woman in chapter 12 is a description of the church of Christ.* **Response:** No! The woman is Israel and her persecution increases in the middle of the future seven year tribulation when the Antichrist breaks his peace treaty with her.

Interpretation: *The flood of water in chapter 12 means the invasions of Barbarians, by which the western empire was overwhelmed. The heathen encouraged their attacks in the hope of destroying Christianity. Another writer states that the same flood of water symbolized a flood of error by which the church of God was in danger of being overwhelmed and carried away.* **Response:** When did this happen in past history? Revelation chapter 12 will occur in the middle of the future seven year tribulation.

Interpretation: *The mark of the beast can be found on the American dime.* **Response:** I looked for quite a long time but I could not find it!

Interpretation: *Different writers presented the following nominations for the False Prophet: The Pope, the Greek Orthodox Church, the French Republic, the Jesuits, heathen philosophy, false doctrine, the principle of inductive philosophy, sin in the*

21

Christian church, witchcraft, and fortune telling. **Response:** How many more different and absurd ideas can writers think of?

Interpretation: *The mark of the beast is observing Sunday.* *Response:* If this is true, I take the Mark of the Beast every Sunday, when I go to church.

Interpretation: *The following men were some of the personalities nominated to be the Antichrist by different writers: A reincarnated Judas Iscariot, Nero, the Pope, an American President, Napoleon, Stalin and other Soviet leaders, Henry Kissinger, Eisenhower, the President of the European Union, the king of Spain, the leader of Syria, a magician in Syria.* *Response:* It was either Hitler or Mussolini when I was a teenager in world war II!

Interpretation: *When the Bible says that the head of the beast was wounded, it means the end of pagan idolatry and the healing of the head was the introduction of Papal idolatry.* *Response:* The beast had six more heads and ten horns. What do they represent?

Interpretation: *The first beast in chapter 13 represents worldly powers and the second beast is a persecuting and assumed power which acts under the disguise of religion and of charity to the souls of men.* *Response:* If I could understand what the writer means by the disguise of religion and of charity to the souls of men I might attempt to respond. The first beast represents the coming Antichrist and the second beast represents his religious leader, the False Prophet. They will both appear in the future.

Interpretation: *Mount Sion in chapter 14 represents the church.*

Response: In chapter 14, Mount Sion is in heaven in the future, but the writer had the church on earth in past history. He did not say when it happened or even what happened.

Interpretation: The 144,000 in heaven in chapter 14 represent the progress of the church Reformation. **Response:** I read chapters 7 and 14 several times, but could not even imagine how the writer could have concluded that the Reformation was involved. The 144,000 Jewish evangelists in heaven in chapter 14 are the same 144,000 Jewish evangelists on earth in chapter 7.

Interpretation: The four living creatures are four ministers from the true church. **Response:** The Bible says that they each had six wings and were full of eyes in front and in back. Each had a different face, one looked like an ox, one looked like a lion, one looked like an eagle, and one looked like a man. I have never seen any minister look like that. Have you?

Interpretation: The river Euphrates drying up to allow the kings of the east to advance to the Battle of Armageddon in chapter 16 means the destruction of the Turkish empire and of idolatry so that a way can be made for the return of the Jews. **Response:** Not so! The Bible says that this was to prepare the kings of the East to march to fight at the Battle of Armageddon in the future.

Interpretation: The beast will reign for 1260 years, not 1260 days. **Response**: That would make the Antichrist older than Methuselah, the oldest man in the Bible.

I could add additional similar illustrations but I have written enough for you to understand how confusing it is for the average reader to know what to believe.

Many of the judgments in Revelation are a repeat of, or similar to, the plagues in Egypt. If the plagues of Egypt were literal, why can't we accept the judgments of the Book of Revelation to be literal also?

3. The Spiritual View

• This view teaches that the Book of Revelation is a story of the ageless spiritual struggle between the forces of good and evil and the ultimate triumph of good.
• Some replacement theology accepts this perspective. I do not.

4. The Futurist View

• This is the most commonly accepted interpretation and is my personal position.
• This view teaches that the Book of Revelation is divided into three divisions (chapter 1 verse 19):

The First Division—Write the Things That You Have Seen
• The Book of Revelation is a recorded vision written by the Apostle John and the first Division is recorded in chapter 1.
• It presents a vision of the glorified Christ.
• It presents seven lampstands which symbolize the seven churches to whom John wrote the vision. The churches were located in Asia Minor.
• The seven churches also represent the entire church age.
• It also presents seven stars which symbolize the seven apostolic pastors of the seven churches.

The Second Division—(Write) the Things Which Are
• This Division is recorded in chapters 2 and 3.
• It presents some of the spiritual history of the seven churches and Christ's messages to them.
• The seven messages are also messages sent to the churches in the entire church age.

The Third Division—(Write) the Things That Will Take Place After This

- The third and final Division records events from the Rapture in chapter 4 verse 1 to the end of the book.
- Chapters 6 to 19 deal with events in heaven and on earth during the reign of the Antichrist in the seven year tribulation. This will climax with the Second Coming of Christ at the Battle of Armageddon. These events are explained as we comment on each chapter.
- Chapters 6 to 19 also describe seven seals of judgment; seven trumpets of judgment and seven bowls of judgment from an angry God.
- These judgments happen consecutively and become more severe as they occur.
- Chapter 19 describes the Marriage Supper of the Lamb, the Second Coming of Christ, the victory of the Battle of Armageddon, the destruction of the Antichrist, the False Prophet, and the judgment on the nations who followed the Antichrist.
- Chapter 20 describes Christ's triumphant reign on the earth for 1,000 years, the imprisonment and the release of the devil, the Great White Throne Judgment of Satan and the unsaved.
- Chapters 21 and 22 describe a new heaven and a new earth with sin and rebellion removed, the New Jerusalem coming down to earth and future eternity.
- Jesus, and many Old Testament writers, predicted the events recorded in the Book of Revelation and this book has more Old Testament references than any other New Testament book.

Now let's begin our journey to discover, verse by verse, the meaning of John's Revelation.

REVELATION:
CHAPTER ONE

In this commentary I am using The New King James Version of the Bible. Regarding the subtitles, I have used some from the NKJV, revised some, and added many of my own to emphasize certain truths.

THE TITLE AND THE THEME

1:1 The Revelation of Jesus Christ, which God gave Him to show His servants things which must shortly take place. And He sent and signified it by His angel to His servant John,

• There are other personalities and events introduced in this interesting and exciting book, but the theme is: the Revelation of Jesus Christ.

• Some Bibles have entitled the book, The Revelation of John the Divine. John was commissioned to write the book, but he wrote about the Revelation of Jesus Christ.

THE MEANING OF REVELATION

• *Revelation* is defined as the unveiling, the uncovering, the enlightening and the clarification. It is used to lift up, or pull back a curtain so that all can see what has been hidden behind the curtain.

• The word, Revelation suggests that God wants to reveal the truth to you and not hide it.

- The book is intended to present to the readers a revelation of the glory of His Majesty, King Jesus and the revelation of coming world events, which will climax with the Battle of Armageddon and the Second Coming of Christ to establish His worldwide Kingdom on earth.
- In one version of the New Testament this book is called The Apocalypse, because the word Revelation is translated from the Greek word *Apokalupsis*.

THE TRANSMISSION OF THE BOOK OF REVELATION

- The Book of Revelation originated with God the Father and was passed from the Father to the Lord Jesus Christ. Jesus gave it to an angel. Thus, this was not only a revelation of Jesus Christ but also a revelation from Him.
- Actually, the angel must have appeared to John as an angel, because when John fell at his feet to worship him, the angel said, *See you do not do that, I am of your fellow servant, the prophets* (Revelation 19:10 and 22:8-9).
- The angel gave the revelation to the Apostle John in a vision and he told John to write down everything he saw.
- John sent the recorded vision to the seven churches (as mentioned in chapters 2 an 3) to the entire church age, and to every believer alive today, so that we could understand the glory and the majesty of the Lord Jesus Christ and the prophecy of future events.

CHRIST IS REVEALED AS PROPHET, PRIEST AND KING

- In the Gospels, Christ was revealed as Prophet during His earthly ministry.
- In the Book of Hebrews, Christ is revealed today as our High Priest.

- The Book of Revelation presents Christ as the King of kings and Lord of lords.

A PROPHECY OF THINGS THAT MUST SHORTLY TAKE PLACE

- The word "shortly" means soon and quickly; there are 45 references to future events in the Book of Revelation.
- The word *prophecy* is mentioned seven times.
- Verse 3 also informs us that the Book of Revelation is a book of future prophecy.
- Out of 404 verses in this book, 350 are prophecy.

EVENTS THAT MUST HAPPEN SOON

- Events that will take place in the history of the seven local churches mentioned.
- Events that will take place in the history of the church from the Day of Pentecost until the Rapture.
- Events that will take place at the resurrection of the righteous dead and the Rapture of the born again living believers.
- Events that will take place in heaven after the Rapture.
- Events that will take place in heaven and on earth during the seven year tribulation.
- Events that will take place in heaven at the celebration of the Marriage Supper of the Lamb at the end of the seven year tribulation.
- Events that will take place when Jesus returns to earth to destroy the Antichrist and his armies at the Battle of Armageddon.
- Events that will take place in the Millennium.
- Events that will take place in future eternity.
- The events occur consecutively in the order they are recorded in the book with some parenthetical passages inserted

between the main events. I will explain the parenthetical passages as we study them.

JOHN, THE WRITER

- John introduces himself as the writer of this book in the first verse. Out of his five books, this is the only one that mentions his name.
- He uses the pronoun, "I" over 70 times in the Book of Revelation, yet in the Gospel of John he does not use the pronoun "I" once.
- John was one of the 12 Apostles.
- He was the brother of James and the son of Zebedee and Salome.
- His mother was one of the women at the cross. She also went to the tomb to anoint the body of Jesus.
- Tradition says that she was a sister of Mary, the mother of Jesus.
- The family had a successful fishing business.
- Salome, John's mother, supported Jesus financially during His earthly ministry (Luke 8:1-3).
- At the time John wrote the Book of Revelation, he was the only one of the original 12 apostles still alive and this was the last book of the Bible to be written.

THE MEANING OF THE WORD "SIGNIFIED"

- Some scholars have suggested that the word *signified* in verse 1 means that John was using the word to imply that he was going to write a book of signs and symbols. However, not all scholars agree.
- The word signified means "showed, pointed out, or announced." Others scholars believe that John was merely writing down the vision as he saw it, or as it was shown to him, announced to him, or pointed out to him.

29

The Authenticity of the Book

1:2 who bore witness to the word of God, and to the testimony of Jesus Christ to all things that he saw.
- The authenticity of the Book of Revelation is based on the Word of God and the testimony of Jesus Christ. This is the Spirit of Prophecy (chapter 19:10).
- The things that John saw in the vision. The word " saw" in the Greek language suggests that John not only saw the personalities and the events in his vision, he also understood the meaning and the truth of what he saw.
- Words suggesting that John saw and recorded a vision are found 45 times in the Book of Revelation.

You Are Blessed as You Read

1:3 Blessed is he who reads and those who hear the words of this prophecy, and keep those things which are written in it; for the time is near.
- There is a blessing promised to (1) the readers of the Book of Revelation, (2) to those who hear the reading of this book, and (3) to those who keep (obey) the things that are written in it.
- As you study this book, continue to remind yourself of this verse and remember you are "blessed" by reading and hearing these words of prophecy.

The Seven Blessings in the Book of Revelation

1. Blessed is he who reads and those who hear the words of this prophecy and keep those things that are written therein (chapter 1:3).
2. Blessed are the dead who die in the Lord (chapter 14:13).

3. Behold I am coming as a thief. Blessed is he who watches and keeps his garments (chapter 16:15).
4. Blessed are they who are called unto the Marriage Supper of the Lamb (chapter 19:9).
5. Blessed and holy is he who has part in the first resurrection (chapter 20:6).
6. Behold I am coming quickly. Blessed is he who keeps the sayings of the prophecy of this book (chapter 22:7).
7. Blessed are they who do His commandments that they may have the right to the tree of life (chapter 22:14).

THE TIME IS NEAR

• Twice in the first three verses and several times throughout the entire book John emphasizes that we are living near the end time.
• Scholars believe John wrote this book in 96 A.D. This means that the end is much nearer now than when John wrote it.

GREETINGS TO THE SEVEN CHURCHES

1:4 John, to the seven churches which are in Asia: Grace to you and peace from Him who is and who was and who is to come, and from the seven Spirits who are before His throne,
• The number seven is repeated 54 times in the Book of Revelation.
• At times it represents the actual number seven.
• At other times it is used to symbolize totality, completeness, wholeness, and perfection.

THE SEVEN CHURCHES

• My wife and I have visited the exact places where these seven churches were located.

- When John refers to Asia, he was not referring to the Continent of Asia, but to Asia Minor, or what we would call the area of Turkey today.
- In the time of the early church, these seven churches were spiritually anointed, thriving, growing congregations, but today nothing remains but ruins.

GRACE AND PEACE

- The phrase "Grace to you" was a common greeting used by the Greeks. "Peace" was used by the Jews.
- John was a Jew but he had ministered in Gentile churches for many years.
- Tradition states that he lived in Ephesus for 20 years, he pastored the church there and was buried there. Thus, he was steeped in both Jewish and Greek culture.
- Using the greetings, grace and peace, he was appealing to both cultures.
- In verse 7, as we will see later, he uses the terms, "Even so, Amen." The Greeks closed their prayers with "Even so" and the Jews with "Amen." Amen means "so be it."
- Grace is God's unmerited and undeserved gift of favor and love. It is receiving what we don't deserve.
- Mercy is not receiving what we do deserve.
- Grace and mercy are two sides of the same coin.
- When we receive the grace of God, we can have peace *with* God. When we have peace with God, we can enjoy the peace *of* God.
- The letters in the word, Grace could stand for: **G**od's **R**iches **A**t **C**hrist's **E**xpense.

SALVATION PAST, PRESENT, AND FUTURE

1:5 and from Jesus Christ, the faithful witness, the firstborn

from the dead and the ruler over the kings of the earth. To Him who loved us and washed (loosed) us from our sins in His own blood,

- Through the blood, we were saved from the penalty of sin.
- Through the blood, we are saved from the power of sin.
- Through the blood, we shall be saved from the presence of sin when Jesus comes.

THE TRINITY IN THE BOOK OF REVELATION

- The word *Trinity* is not found in the Bible but the truth of the Triune Godhead is clearly taught.
- In chapter 1 verse 4, there is a reference to God the eternal Father. In the same verse we also read of the 7 Spirits. This is a reference to the Holy Spirit, another member of the Trinity.
- Verse 5 presents Jesus again. This completes the Trinity.
- There are not seven Holy Spirits. There is only one Spirit (Ephesians 4:4) and seven is the number of perfection.
- Thus, the Holy Spirit is perfect, total, and complete.
- The book of Isaiah 11:2 refers to seven attributes of the Holy Spirit:
  1. The Spirit of the Lord.
  2. The Spirit of wisdom.
  3. The Spirit of understanding.
  4. The Spirit of counsel.
  5. The Spirit of might.
  6. The Spirit of knowledge.
  7. The Spirit of the fear of the Lord.

GOD'S THRONE IN HEAVEN

The throne is mentioned at least 40 times in the Book of Revelation. It is the center of all the activities of heaven.

CHRIST, THE FIRSTBORN FROM THE DEAD

- The Scriptures refer to Jesus as the only begotten Son five times. That is when He was born at Bethlehem.
- The Bible also refers to Him as the firstborn or the "first born from the dead" five times. This refers to His resurrection.
- The first Adam experienced sin in paradise and the second Adam, Jesus, experienced righteousness in Hades.
- Jesus was the first person to be born again. He was born again in Hades and since His resurrection He has welcomed many brothers and sisters into the family of God.

RULER OVER THE KINGS OF THE EARTH

- This is a prophetic insert.
- Jesus has the authority to reign as King of kings today, but He will not do so until He defeats the Antichrist at the Battle of Armageddon.
- This is when He returns to reign on the earth at His Second Coming.

NEW CREATION REALITIES

1:6 and has made us kings and priests to His God and Father, to Him be glory and dominion forever and ever. Amen.
In verses 4, 5, and 6 we have a record of the following new creation realities:

- Grace—The unearned and undeserved favor of God. Love gifts received freely from God by faith.
- Peace—Freedom from all inner turmoil, past, present, and future.
- He loved us—with an eternal, unconditional love.
- He washed us (or loosed us) from our sins in His own blood.

HE MADE US PROPHETS, PRIESTS, AND KINGS

- As prophets we minister to one another and we witness to the lost.
- As priests we minister to the Lord in thanksgiving, praise and worship.
- As kings we have power and authority over the enemy (Luke 10:19).

JESUS COMES IN CLOUDS

1:7 Behold, He is coming with clouds, and every eye will see Him, even they who pierced Him. And all the tribes of the earth will mourn because of Him. Even so, Amen.
- When Jesus ascended back to heaven He went in a cloud (Acts 1:9).
- When He comes in the air for His saints at the Rapture, He will come in a cloud (1 Thessalonians 4:17).
- When He comes back to earth with His saints to fight at the Battle of Armageddon, He will come with clouds (verse 7).
- The promise of Christ's return is recorded three times in the Book of Revelation, in chapter 1, chapter 11, and chapter 19.

EVERY EYE WILL SEE JESUS

- When Jesus returns to the earth with His Bride to fight His enemies at the Battle of Armageddon every eye will see Him.
- But not every eye will see Him when He comes to the clouds for His Bride at the Rapture.
- There will be a special outpouring of grace on the people who pierced Him, the Jews (Zechariah 12:10).
- The Jews will ask Him where He received the nail wounds in His hands (Zechariah 12:10 and 13:6).

- He will reply, I received them in the house of My friends (Zechariah 13:6).
- Verse 7 also declares that all the tribes of the earth will mourn because of Him.
- Some Bible scholars believe that John was referring to all the tribes of Israel rather than all the nations of the earth.
- The Greek word for mourn means to wail in an impassioned expression of grief.

JESUS IS THE ETERNAL GOD

1:8 "I am the Alpha and the Omega, the Beginning and the End," says the Lord, who "is and who was and who is to come, the Almighty."
- This verse confirms that Jesus Christ is the eternal, Almighty God.
- The word Almighty is used of God 48 times in the Old Testament.
- The alpha and the omega are the first and last letters of the Greek alphabet.
- In the Hebrew language, the language of the Old Testament, it reads, I am the *alef* and the *tav*.
- The symbol of the *alef* is an ox and the symbol of the *tav* is a cross.
- The Old Covenant began with animal sacrifice and ended with the cross.
- This verse also gives lie to the cults which teach that Jesus is a lesser god.

JOHN EXILED ON PATMOS

1:9 "I, John, both your brother and companion in the tribulation and kingdom and patience of Jesus Christ, was on the island that is called Patmos for the Word of God and for the testimony of Jesus Christ."

• When John wrote the Book of Revelation, the New Testament Church was experiencing great persecution by the Roman Emperors.
• John was a fellow sufferer in this persecution.
• All of the 12 Apostles except John had been killed as martyrs.
• Some early traditions state that John had been boiled alive in oil and survived.
• He was banished to the Island of Patmos where he saw the vision of the Book of Revelation and recorded his vision.
• The Isle of Patmos was a small, volcanic, rocky and lonely island located in the Aegean Sea off the coast of Turkey. It was barren and had no trees or vegetation.
• Patmos was approximately ten miles long and six miles wide, and was located about 30 miles southwest of Ephesus and was a prison camp for the worst kind of criminals.
• John's only crime was that he was a Christian.

JOHN'S VISION OF JESUS ON THE LORD'S DAY

1:10 "I was in the Spirit on the Lord's Day and I heard behind me a loud voice, as of a trumpet,
• Bible scholars do not all agree on the meaning of the Lord's Day.
• Some teach that John had this Spiritual revelation on Sunday, the Lord's Day.
• Others believe that he was taken in the Spirit to a period of time in the future which had been prophesied more than 30 times in the Old and New Testaments as, the Day of the Lord.
• It is also called, the great and terrible Day of the Lord.
• The Day of the Lord is the day of God's coming judgment.
• Scholars who hold to this view believe that the verse should be translated, *I was in the Spirit in the Lord's Day.*
• Because the Bible does not tell us what John meant by the Lord's Day, we will not speculate further.

JOHN'S COMMISSION TO WRITE THIS BOOK TO SEVEN CHURCHES

1:11 saying, 'I am the Alpha and the Omega, the First and the Last,' and, 'What you see, write in a book and send it to the seven churches which are in Asia: to Ephesus, to Smyrna, to Pergamos, to Thyatira, to Sardis, to Philadelphia, and to Laodicea.'

- Although the Bible refers to a book, it was a scroll.
- It was written to the seven churches mentioned.
- The message is also for the church of all ages and we read in verse 3 that the book (scroll) was written to every believer.
- Some theologians believe that each church represents a period of time in church history. However, there is no Scripture to support this teaching.

A DESCRIPTION OF JESUS

1:12 "Then I turned to see the voice that spoke with me. And having turned I saw seven golden lampstands,

- John turned to see the voice that spoke.
- Usually one listens to a voice.
- John must have been so awed by the presence of the Lord that when he heard His voice, he turned to see the One who spoke.

THE SEVEN GOLDEN LAMPSTANDS

- These lampstands are mentioned seven times in the Book of Revelation. Verse 20 explains that the seven lampstands probably a menorah) represent the seven churches.
- Jesus said that the church must be the light of the world (John 5:14). He also stated, *Let your light so shine before men, that they may see your good works, and glorify your Father which is in heaven* (John 5:16).

38

THE VISION OF THE SON OF MAN

1:13 and in the midst of the seven lampstands One like the Son of Man, clothed with a garment down to the feet and girded about the chest with a golden band.

14 His head and hair were white like wool, as white as snow, and His eyes like a flame of fire;

15 His feet were like fine brass, as if refined in a furnace, and His voice as the sound of many waters;

16 He had in His right hand seven stars, out of His mouth went a sharp two-edged sword, and His countenance was like the sun shining in its strength.

- In chapters 2 and 3, as Christ sends messages to each of the seven churches, He mentions these same descriptive characteristics again, one by one.

CHRIST STANDING IN THE MIDST OF THE LAMPSTAND

- We see Christ is standing in the midst of the seven lampstands, the seven churches.
- His garments speak of royalty because He is the King of kings.
- Because there were many more than seven churches in Asia Minor at this time, we conclude that the number seven symbolizes the total and complete church.

SYMBOLS OF JUDGMENT

The following descriptions of Christ symbolize judgment:
- His eyes were like a flame of fire.
- His feet were like fine brass, as if refined in a furnace.
- His voice (was like) the sound of many waters.
- Out of His mouth went a sharp two-edged sword.
- His countenance was like the sun shining in its strength.

The Seven Stars

- The seven stars symbolize the seven pastors of the seven churches. They are held in the right hand of Christ.
- The right hand represents blessing, power and authority.

John's Reaction to His Vision of the Glorified Christ

1:17 And when I saw Him, I fell at His feet as dead. But He laid His right hand on me, saying to me, "Do not be afraid; I am the First and the Last."

- At the Last Supper, John laid his head on the shoulder of Jesus.
- During His earthly ministry, John and Jesus were close friends. In fact, John is called, the disciple whom Jesus loved.
- When John saw the glorified Christ, he was afraid and fell at His feet as dead.
- Jesus reassured John and told him not to be afraid.
- Today Jesus is our Savior and friend but when we meet Him at the Judgment Seat, He will be our Judge.
- John was the same writer who wrote in his Epistles, *And now little children, abide in Him, that when He appears, we may have confidence and not be ashamed before Him at His coming* (1 John 2:28).

Christ Has the Keys of Hades and Death

1:18 "I am He who lives, and was dead, and behold, I am alive forevermore. Amen. And I have the keys of Hades and of Death."

- Christ died, was buried, and rose again to live eternally.
- During His earthly ministry, Jesus laid aside His Divine attributes and was confined to the limitations of a physical body.

- He could be in one place only at one time.
- Now He is the eternal God with all His Divine attributes restored.
- The word Amen is the same word as verily. The word means "so be it" and confirms that Christ is alive eternally.

KEYS ARE A SYMBOL OF POWER AND AUTHORITY

- Christ the living and eternal King has power and authority over Hades and Death. Hades is translated hell in the KJV.
- Hades was the place where the souls and spirits of the dead went before Jesus died on the cross.
- Hades has two compartments with a great, impassible gulf between them.
- One compartment is for the souls of the lost.
- It is a place of fire, a place of torment, a place of consciousness and a place of memory.
- The other compartment is called paradise. It is for the souls of the righteous.

THE RICH MAN AND LAZARUS

- Jesus told about the rich man and Lazarus the beggar in Luke 16:19–31.
- The rich man died and went to Hades, the place of torment.
- The beggar died and went to paradise. This compartment was also called, Abraham's bosom.
- When Jesus was crucified, His body was placed in the tomb but His soul and spirit went to Hades.
- Jesus had to take the sinner's place and with the sin of the world, Jesus went to the place of torment. Then, when the demands of Divine justice had been satisfied and Jesus had suffered the torments of the damned, His spirit was born again.

41

- As God Almighty, He snatched the keys of Hades and Death from the devil and used them to liberate the souls of the righteous in the paradise portion of Hades.
- That is when He led captivity captive (Ephesians 4:8).

SOME OLD TESTAMENT SAINTS RESURRECTED WITH JESUS

- In Matthew 27:52-53 the Bible records that when Jesus rose from the dead there were many Old Testament saints who were also raised from the dead and were seen walking the streets of Jerusalem.
- These were some of the saints who had been in the paradise compartment of Hades before Christ's resurrection.
- Since the resurrection, the paradise compartment of Hades is empty.
- Today, when the saved die they go immediately to paradise which is now in heaven.
- When the unsaved die, their spirits and souls still go to the torment compartment of Hades awaiting the Great White Throne Judgment when Death and Hades will be cast into the Lake of Fire (Revelation 20:14).

THE THREE DIVISIONS OF THE BOOK

1:19 Write the things which you have seen, and the things which are, and the things which will take place after this.
- We explained the three divisions as we examined the Fourth Interpretation in the Overview.

THE SEVEN STARS AND THE SEVEN LAMPSTANDS EXPLAINED

1:20 The mystery of the seven stars which you saw in My right

***hand, and the seven golden lampstands: The seven stars
are the angels (pastors) of the seven churches.***
- We have already explained the symbolism of the seven stars.
  They are the apostolic pastors of the seven churches.
- Tradition records that there was a Roman Emperor whose son
  died in 85 A.D.
- The emperor minted a coin of his son holding seven stars.
- The seven stars were symbolic of his having power over the
  seven continents.
- There is no record in history of any Roman Emperor's son
  ruling the world, but what John saw prophetically will
  certainly come to pass.
- Peter said that we also have a more sure word of prophecy
  (2 Peter 1:19).

Revelation:
Chapter Two

In this chapter we find a threefold application of Christ's messages:

1. There is a local application to each of the seven churches mentioned.
2. There is a prophetical application to all the churches in the entire church age.
3. There is a personal application given to every believer because the Bible states, *He who has an ear, let him hear what the Spirit says to the churches.*

2:1 "To the angel (pastor) of the church of Ephesus write, 'These things says He who holds the seven stars in His right hand, who walks in the midst of the seven golden lampstands:"

The Angel of the Church

- The word angel means messenger. It refers to the pastor of the church.
- Each letter is addressed to the angel of the church.

Historical Background of Ephesus

- Ephesus was at one time an important, magnificent city that was a center of trade and the seat of government. It had a temple and its hanging gardens were among the seven wonders of the ancient world.

- The church in Ephesus was founded by Paul. He stayed there for two years and the church grew spiritually and numerically.
- The interesting story of the origin of the church is recorded in Acts chapter 19.
- The Bible states that Paul performed special miracles in Ephesus.
- The Epistle of the Ephesians was a letter Paul later wrote to the church.
- After Paul had founded the church, Timothy pastored there.
- Tradition states that the Apostle John also pastored the church at Ephesus and that he lived there for 20 years and was buried there.
- Unfortunately, this thriving church, which had several things that Christ commended, lost its first love and the message Christ gave to the church was to repent.
- How sad that Jesus is seen walking in the midst of the seven churches when He wrote to the first church, the church at Ephesus. But when you read the letter to the last church, the church of Laodicea, Christ was outside the church, knocking at the door asking for an invitation to enter.

SPIRITUAL QUALITIES CHRIST COMMENDS

2:2 "I know your works, your labor, your patience, and that you cannot bear those who are evil. And you have tested those who say they are apostles and are not, and have found them liars;

3 and you have persevered and have patience, and have labored for My name's sake and have not become weary."

- Jesus commends the church for their works and their labors. In the Greek, the word labor is a much more demanding word than work. The church was lauded for:

- Their patience.
- Their stand against evil.
- Their opposition to false apostles.
- Their perseverance—they did not become weary.

CHRIST'S CONDEMNATION OF THE CHURCH

2:4 *"Nevertheless I have this against you, that you have left your first love."*
- Jesus condemns the church because they had left their first love.
- This may be the condition of some churches today. They may sing the right hymns, pray the right prayers, and go through the right religious motions, yet they have left their first love.

THE MEANING OF LOVE

- In the English language there is only one word for love.
- We say, I love my wife; I love my dog; I love my car; I love my job and I love Jesus. On the other hand, there are several words in the Greek language to describe love:

  Eros is the word for physical love. We get the English word, erotic from this word.

  Phileo is the word used for brotherly love or friendship love. The city of Philadelphia is the city of brotherly love.

  Agape is the word for the God kind of love. Only born again believers can have agape love.
- When Jesus told the church at Ephesus that they had left their first love, He used the word agape. And He used the same word in Matthew 24:12 concerning the last days. He said, *the love (agape) of many will grow cold.*
- Love is not an emotion, it is a decision.
- Emotion is the byproduct of love.

- Love is a sacrificial choice that seeks the highest and the best for the one who is the object of our love.
- Love is the badge of discipleship (John 13:35).
- The very nature of God is love (1 John 4:8).

A CALL TO REPENTANCE

2:5 "Remember therefore from where you have fallen; repent and do the first works, or else I will come to you quickly and remove your lampstand from its place—unless you repent."

- Jesus calls the church to repent.
- Repentance is a message for the saved and the unsaved.
- Jesus uses the word "repent" seven times in the Book of Revelation and the message is always addressed to the church.
- The word Repent means to change your mind, change your attitude and change your behavior.

GOD HATES THE SECT OF THE NICOLAITANS

2:6 "But this you have, that you hate the deeds of the Nicolaitans, which I also hate."

- The Nicolaitans was a sect that taught immorality was not sin.
- The men married a plurality of wives and they taught that eating food which had been offered to idols was acceptable, even though the church had condemned it in Acts 15.
- The Ephesian church was opposed to this false teaching and Christ commended them.

THE PROMISE IS TO THE OVERCOMER

2:7 "He who has an ear, let him hear what the Spirit says to the churches. To him who overcomes I will give to eat from

the tree of life, which is in the midst of the Paradise of God."

- The message of Christ to the churches is that the promises are only for the overcomer.
- Christ's first promise to the overcomer is the tree of life.
- The tree of life was first placed in the Garden of Eden.
- After Adam's sin, God drove man out of the garden because had he eaten of the tree of life he would have lived forever in a sinful condition.
- Now the tree of life is in heaven.
- In future eternity, the tree of life will be on the banks of the river of life that flows from the New Jerusalem (chapter 22:1-2).
- Because the tree of life in heaven is promised only to the overcomer, it can be concluded that only the overcoming Christians will go to heaven.

CHRIST'S MESSAGE TO THE CHURCH OF SMYRNA

2:8 "And to the angel (pastor) of the church in Smyrna write, 'These things says the First and the Last, who was dead, and came to life:'"

- Smyrna was a wealthy city, located about 50 miles southwest of Ephesus.
- The city is now called Ismir in Turkey.

JESUS COMMENDS THE CHURCH

2:9 "I know your works, tribulation and poverty (but you are rich); and I know the blasphemy of those who say they are Jews and are not, but are of the synagogue of Satan.

10 Do not fear any of those things which you are about to suffer. Indeed, the devil is about to throw some of you into prison, that you may be tested, and you will have

tribulation ten days. Be faithful until death, and I will give you the crown of life."
- Christ commends the church at Smyrna for their works, for their tribulation, and for their poverty.
- Jesus said that they were rich spiritually.

CHRIST CONDEMNS SPIRITUAL COMPROMISE

- The church at Smyrna was condemned because some did not practice what they preached, and others were compromising with Satan worship.
- There was a sect in Smyrna who professed to be Jews but who served Satan.
- Apparently, there were some members of the church in Smyrna who were fellowshipping with this sect. Jesus called them the synagogue of Satan.
- Christ condemns the church for compromising with Satan worship.

THE MOVIE, THE EXORCIST

- It is dangerous for anyone to make contact with the kingdom of darkness.
- Several years ago there was a film released called *The Exorcist*. A few of our church members went to see the movie and afterwards some of them could not sleep at night because they were seeing things or sensing a presence in the bedroom or hearing voices.
- Pauline prayed deliverance for several of them—and it brought them into freedom.

JESUS ENCOURAGES THE CHURCH

- Christ warns the church of coming persecution and He encourages them not to fear.

- He informs them that some members of the church would be thrown into prison and perhaps even killed for their faith.
- With the warning, Jesus encourages them not to fear and to be faithful unto death.

CHRIST PROMISES THE OVERCOMER A CROWN OF LIFE

YES

- The New Testament mentions five crowns for the overcoming believers. They include:
    1. The incorruptible crown (1 Corinthians 9:25).
    2. The crown of rejoicing (1 Thessalonians 2:19).
    3. The crown of righteousness (2 Timothy 4:8).
    4. The crown of glory (1 Peter 5:6).
    5. The crown of life (Revelation 2:10).

LOGOS AND RHEMA

2:11 *"He who has an ear, let him hear what the Spirit says to the churches. He who overcomes shall not be hurt by the second death."*

- In the Greek language, the language of the New Testament, there are two translations of "word." *Logos* means the written word. *Rhema* means the spoken word.
- The Holy Spirit takes the Logos of the Scriptures and gives to each of us a clear, personal Rhema word.
- To each church, Christ emphasizes that hearing the Rhema Word made real by the Holy Spirit is important, even necessary, to live the overcoming life.

A PERSONAL PROMISE OF CHILDREN

- An illustration of the relationship between Logos and Rhema happened to my wife, Pauline.

- She had lost four children with miscarriages and four doctors told her that it was physically impossible for her to have any children.
- In the hospital room, after she had lost her fourth baby, she cried out to God, "Lord have you forgotten all about me?"
- The Lord prompted her to open her Bible and the Logos became Rhema. She read, *"Can a woman forget her sucking child? ...Yet, I will not forget thee...The children which thou shalt have, after thou hast lost the others"* (Isaiah 49:15,20 KJV).
- How appropriate! God had spoken to her personally. She felt impressed to open her Bible repeatedly and read seven different verses. All the verses were promises that God would give her children The seventh Scripture said, *"Then you will say to yourself, 'Who gave me all these children?'"* (Isaiah 49:21 NCV).
- We had four children in four years (three within 18 months)!
- To other people the seven verses Pauline read would have been Logos but the Holy Spirit made Logos become Rhema to her.

THE OVERCOMERS WILL NOT BE HURT BY THE SECOND DEATH

- Christ clearly teaches that only overcoming Christians will not be hurt by the second death.
- The second death describes the eternal Lake of Fire (chapter 20:14).
- Death in the Bible means separation.
- The second death refers to separation from God for all eternity.

THE CHURCH AT PERGAMOS AND THE TWO-EDGED SWORD

2:12 And to the angel (pastor) of the church in Pergamos

51

write, *"These things says He who has the sharp two-edged sword."*

- Pergamos was a city in Mysia on the river Caicus about 50 miles north of Smyrna.
- The fact that Christ introduces Himself as the One with the two–edged sword, suggests He had some things that He planned to judge in the church.

CHRIST COMMENDS THE CHURCH AT PERGAMOS

2:13 "I know your works and where you dwell, where Satan's throne is, And you hold fast in My name, and did not deny My faith even in the days in which Antipas was My faithful martyr, who was killed among you, where Satan dwells."

- Christ commends the members of this church for their works and commitment to Him even though they lived in the midst of satanic influence.
- They did not deny their faith in Christ even though Antipas, their pastor, had been martyred by Satan worshippers.
- Tradition states that Antipas was martyred for his faith by being placed in a blazing fire that was burning inside a brazen bull.
- There is a Book of Antipas which is not included in the cannon of Scripture.

CHRIST CONDEMNS THE CHURCH AT PERGAMOS

2:14 "But I have a few things against you, because you have there those who hold the doctrine of Balaam, who taught Balack to put a stumbling block before the children of Israel, to eat things sacrificed to idols, and to commit sexual immorality.

15 Thus you also have those who hold the doctrine of the Nicolaitans, which things I hate. "
- We learned that the Church at Ephesus took a strong stand against the doctrine of the Nicolaitans.
- The church at Pergamos was guilty of accepting and practicing both the doctrine of Balaam and the doctrine of the Nicolaitans. The two doctrines were very similar.

CHRIST CALLS THE CHURCH TO REPENTANCE

2:16 "Repent, or else I will come to you quickly and will fight against them with the sword of My mouth. "
- The Book of Hebrews teaches that the spoken Word of Christ has the constructive power to create and uphold the universe.
- His spoken Word also has the destructive power to destroy His enemies.
- When Christ comes again, He will destroy the Antichrist and the nations who ally with him with a symbolic sword out of His mouth (chapter 19:15).
- Some sins Christ will deal with on Judgment Day, but here Jesus says, *Repent or else I will come to you quickly and will fight against those who commit the sins mentioned.*

A LISTENING EAR

2:17 "He who has an ear, let him hear what the Spirit says to the churches. To him who overcomes I will give some of the hidden manna to eat. And I will give him a white stone, and on the stone a new name written which no one knows except him who receives it. "
- Every believer who attends church listens to the Word of God, but does not necessarily listen with an attentive ear.
- Christ expects us to have a listening ear.
- The word "hear" means not only to listen but to obey.

The Promise of Hidden Manna to the Overcomer

- Manna was the miracle food God provided for Israel in the wilderness.
- Many of the early Christians were being persecuted and were deprived of food and drink.
- Promising manna for the overcomer was God's way of assuring them of His miracle provision.

The Promise of a White Stone

- Jesus also promised the overcomer a white stone—which was also called a "victory stone."
- In John's day Judges would give a white stone or a black stone to the people on trial.
- If they received a black stone they were guilty and condemned.
- If they received a white stone they were innocent and released.
- Thank God our sins are forgiven. We have no guilt nor condemnation. We will receive a white stone.

The Compromising Church of Thyatira

2:18 *"And to the angel (pastor) of the church in Thyatira write, 'These things says the Son of God, who has eyes like a flame of fire, and His feet like fine brass:'"*
- Thyatira was a city in west Turkey, located between Pergamos and Sardis.

Christ the Judge

- The eyes of Christ were like a flame of fire.

- His feet were like fine brass.
- This description of Christ symbolizes judgment.

CHRIST COMMENDS THE CHURCH AT THYATIRA

2:19 "I know your works, love, service, faith, and your patience; and as for your works, the last are more than the first."
- Jesus commends the church at Thyatira for five things:
    1. Their works. We are not saved by works, but we are saved *to* work.
    2. Their love. This must be the method, the motivation and the message of all our works and service.
    3. Their service.
    4. Their faith.
    5. Their patience.

CHRIST CONDEMNS THE CHURCH FOR ACCEPTING JEZEBEL

2:20 "Nevertheless I have a few things against you, because you allow that woman Jezebel, who calls herself a prophetess, to teach and seduce My servants to commit sexual immorality and eat things sacrificed to idols.
21 And I gave her time to repent of her sexual immorality, and she did not repent.
22 Indeed I will cast her into a sickbed, and those who commit adultery with her into great tribulation, unless they repent of their deeds.
23 And I will kill her children with death, and all the churches shall know that I am He who searches the minds and hearts. And I will give to each one of you according to your works."
- Christ condemns the church for allowing a false prophetess named Jezebel to minister.

- They allowed her to seduce church members to commit immorality and to influence Christians to eat food that had been offered to idols.
- God gave Jezebel time to repent and because she did not, He judged her, her family and those she had seduced.
- Although the woman died almost 2,000 years ago, the Jezebel spirit is very much alive today.
- Because it is a spirit, it can operate in men and women.
- I have known pastors and wives, elders, deacons, and church members with that spirit. And I have also known wives, mothers, husbands, and fathers who control their families with that spirit.
- Sadly, I have also seen children who control parents with the Jezebel spirit.

WE ENCOUNTERED THE JEZEBEL SPIRIT

- When God called my wife and me to plant a church in my home town in England, Pauline asked God what strongholds we would face in that city.
- God answered her prayer and said, among other strongholds we would encounter the spirit of Jezebel.
- One woman with that spirit bragged how she had been kicked out of every church she had attended for the past 20 years. The spirit of Jezebel, working through her, tried to ruin our church.

AHAB AND JEZEBEL

- The first Jezebel was the wife of a weak king named Ahab in Elijah's day.
- She killed the true prophets of God and attacked Elijah so viciously that Elijah wanted to die.
- Today, whenever you have an Elijah anointing behind the pulpit, look for a Jezebel spirit in the pew.

SOME MEMBERS REMAINED TRUE

2:24 "Now to you I say, and to the rest in Thyatira, as many as do not have this doctrine, who have not known the depths of Satan, as they say, I will put on you no other burden."
- Gnostics, people who pursue and share mystical and occult knowledge, taught a doctrine called, the depths of God.
- Jesus called it the depths of Satan.

HOLD FAST AND OVERCOME

2:25 "But hold fast what you have till I come.
26 And he who overcomes, and keeps My works until the end, to him I will give power over the nations
27 "He shall rule them with a rod of iron; They shall be dashed to pieces like the potter's vessels as I also have received from My Father;
28 and I will give him the morning star.
29 He who has an ear, let him hear what the Spirit says to the churches."
- Christ commands the church to hold fast, to remain faithful, to persevere, and to live in the light of Christ's soon return.

THE PROMISE TO THE OVERCOMERS

- They will rule with Christ over the nations of the earth.
- This will happen after Jesus comes back to fight at the Battle of Armageddon to destroy His enemies and to establish His worldwide Kingdom on earth.

WHO WILL REIGN WITH CHRIST?

- The saints of all ages. They will be resurrected and raptured when Jesus returns to the air. I believe that this event will occur before the seven year tribulation begins.
- The 144,000 Jewish evangelists (chapters 7 and 14).
- The two witnesses (chapter 11).
- The tribulation martyrs (chapter 20:4).

ADDITIONAL PROMISES TO THE OVERCOMERS

- Jesus promises the overcoming Christian the morning star— the person of Christ Himself (chapter 22:16).
- Verse 27 is a prophetic quotation from Psalm 2:9 concerning our authority to reign in Christ's future Kingdom.

REVELATION:
CHAPTER THREE

Christ does not hesitate to condemn wrongdoing in the churches, but as we will see, He also makes promises to the overcomers.

3:1 "And to the angel (pastor) of the church in Sardis write, 'These things says He who has the seven Spirits of God and the seven stars: I know your works, that you have a name that you are alive, but you are dead.'"
- Sardis was a city about 40 miles east of Smyrna.
- It was the ancient capital of Lydia.

THE SEVEN SPIRITS OF GOD

- In chapter 1 we learned that there is only one Holy Spirit and the number seven refers to the Spirit's totality, completeness and perfection.
- Some have also taught that it suggests God has power and authority over, and knowledge of, the seven continents and thus, He rules over the whole wide world.

CHRISTIANS AT SARDIS HAD A NAME TO LIVE BY BUT THEY WERE DEAD

- This could be true of some churches today. They may call themselves Christians, but when Jesus was speaking of the last days, He said, *"Many will say to Me in that day, 'Lord,*

Lord, have we not prophesied in Your name, cast out demons in Your name, and done many mighty works in Your name? And then I will declare to them, 'I never knew you; depart from Me, you who practice lawlessness!" (Matthew 7:22–23).
- What an indictment! Will Christ say that of you and me?

Warning

CHRIST'S CONDEMNATION AND CHALLENGES

3:2 "Be watchful, and strengthen the things which remain, that are ready to die, for I have not found your works perfect before God.

3 Remember therefore how you have received and heard; hold fast and repent. Therefore if you will not watch, I will come upon you as a thief, and you will not know what hour I will come upon you."
- Although there were a few in the church who were alive spiritually, Christ condemns and challenges the majority in the church because their works were not acceptable.
- They were spiritually dead and He demanded a greater commitment and obedience.
- He told them to be spiritually revived and become strong in the Lord.
- He encouraged them to hold fast.
- He commanded them to repent.
- He warned them to remember the truth they had been taught.
- He told them to watch for they did not know the hour of Christ's coming. Jesus will come as a thief without warning.

PROMISES TO THE OVERCOMER

3:4 "You have a few names even in Sardis who have not defiled their garments; and they shall walk with Me in white, for they are worthy.

60

5 He who overcomes shall be clothed in white garments, and I will not blot out his name from the Book of Life; but I will confess his name before My Father and before His angels.

6 He who has an ear, let him hear what the Spirit says to the churches."

- Christ commends the overcomers who had not defiled their garments.
- He promises that they will walk with Him in white.
- Repeatedly, Christ offers eternal rewards, and even eternal life only to the overcomer.
- Additional promises include, white garments (which symbolize righteousness).
- Christ will not blot out their names from the Book of Life.
- From this verse, it seems obvious, that people who are not overcomers can have their names removed from the Book of Life.
- Names cannot be removed from the Book of Life unless they are first recorded there.
- Christ will confess their names before the Father and the angels of heaven.
- Salvation is called the great confession.
- We confess Christ before men on earth. He confesses us before the Father and before the angels in heaven.

THE PROMISE TO THE FAITHFUL CHURCH OF PHILADELPHIA

3:7 "And to the angel (pastor) of the church in Philadelphia write, 'These things says He who is holy, He who is true, He who has the key of David, He who opens and no one shuts, and shuts and no one opens.'"

- Philadelphia was a city about 30 miles southeast of Sardis.

61

CHRIST HAS THE KEY OF DAVID

- Keys are a symbol of power and authority.
- Jesus was saying that He had all the power and authority the Old Testament Scriptures had ever prophesied about the promised Messiah, the Son of David.

IS THE OPEN DOOR THE RAPTURE?

3:8 *"I know your works. See, I have set before you an open door, and no one can shut it for you have a little strength, have kept My word, and have not denied My name."*
- Some scholars believe that verse 8 refers to the open door of the Rapture.
- They also believe that verse 10 promises that the overcoming believer will not go through the seven year tribulation.

QUALITIES FOR WHICH JESUS COMMENDS THE CHURCH

- Their works.
- Their strength.
- Their obedience.
- Their faith.
- Their faithfulness.
- They had not denied Christ's Name.

CHRIST PROMISES JUDGMENT

3:9 *"Indeed I will make those of the synagogue of Satan, who say they are Jews and are not, but lie—indeed I will make them come and worship before your feet, and to know that I have loved you."*

- He will expose all liars and humble them before the church.
- Christ will confirm His love for the church before the liars.

CHRIST PROMISES PROTECTION

3:10 "Because you have kept My command to persevere, I also will keep you from the hour of trial which shall come upon the whole world, to test those who dwell on the earth."
- Because the church had been obedient and had persevered, Christ promises that He would preserve them from future tribulation.

3:11 "Behold, I am coming quickly! Hold fast what you have, that no one may take your crown."
- The soon return of Christ and the need for the believer to be ready is mentioned several times throughout the Book of Revelation.
- They are repeatedly encouraged to hold fast.
- Believers are also warned that they could lose their crown, which is their reward to reign with Christ in His coming Kingdom.

ADDITIONAL PROMISES FOR THE OVERCOMER

3:12 "He who overcomes, I will make him a pillar in the temple of My God, and he shall go out no more. I will write on him the name of My God and the name of the city of My God, the New Jerusalem, which comes down out of heaven from My God. And I will write on him My new name."
- The overcomer will be a pillar in the temple in heaven.
- Three different names will be written on the overcoming believer. They are: The Name of God, the Father; the name of the city of God, the New Jerusalem; My New Name, the new Name of Christ.

3:13 He who has an ear let him hear what the Spirit says to the churches.

The Condemnation of the Lukewarm Church of Laodicea

3:14 And to the angel (pastor) of the church of the Laodiceans write, "These things says the Amen, the Faithful and True Witness, the Beginning of the creation of God:"

- Laodicea was a prosperous city of trade and banking located a few miles west of Colosse. It became an important medical center.
- The Apostle Paul refers to the Church in Laodicea when he wrote to the Church in Colosse.

The Beginning of the Creation of God

- This does not teach that Christ was the first person created by God because Christ had no beginning. He is a member of the eternal Godhead.
- It means that Christ Himself created all things from the beginning.
- The Bible declares, *All things were made by Him; and without Him was not anything made that was made* (John 1:3).

Not Hot Nor Cold

3:15 "I know your works, that you are neither cold nor hot. I could wish you were cold or hot."

- Christ condemns the church of the Laodiceans because they were neither cold nor hot.
- Unfortunately, this is the condition of many professing Christians today.

LUKEWARM CHRISTIANS MAKE CHRIST SICK

3:16 "So then, because you are lukewarm, and neither cold nor hot, I will vomit you out of My mouth."
• This should be a warning to all of us.
• Either we are part of the overcoming church of Philadelphia, who will make the Rapture or we belong to the lukewarm church of Laodicea, who will miss the Rapture and go through the seven year tribulation.

THE LUKEWARM CHURCH WAS SELF SUFFICIENT

3:17 Because you say, "I am rich, have become wealthy, and have need of nothing"—and do not know that you are wretched, miserable, poor, blind, and naked.
• The lukewarm Christians saw themselves as wealthy, self sufficient, needing nothing.

CHRIST SAW THE LUKEWARM CHURCH AS SPIRITUALLY POOR

• Jesus saw this church as deplorable—wretched, miserable, poor, blind, and naked.

CHRIST COUNSELS THE CHURCH

3:18 "I counsel you to buy from Me gold refined in the fire, that you may be rich; and white garments, that you may be clothed, that the shame of your nakedness may not be revealed; and anoint your eyes with eye salve, that you may see."
• In 1 Corinthians 3:12-13, Paul refers to our works and our rewards as gold burned in the fire.
• White garments are mentioned repeatedly in the Book of Revelation. They refer to righteousness.

- We have to conclude from this verse that members of the lukewarm church had lost their white garments of righteousness because Jesus accused them of being naked.
- If they were in the church at one time they had to be clothed in white robes of righteousness, but they had lost them.
- Jesus commanded them to buy them and be clothed.
- Salvation is free, but the Bible states that the truth must be bought (Proverbs 23:23).
- Only the truth makes us free (John 8:32).
- Eye salve refers to understanding and revelation (Psalm 19:8).

GRACE IN A TIME OF JUDGMENT

3:19 "As many as I love, I rebuke and chasten. Therefore be zealous and repent."
- In all of the Lord's judgments we see His grace calling men to repentance.

3:20 "Behold, I stand at the door and knock. If anyone hears My voice and opens the door, I will come in to him and dine with him, and he with Me.
21 To him who overcomes I will grant to sit with Me on My throne, as I also overcame and sat down with My Father on His throne.
22 He who has an ear, let him hear what the Spirit says to the churches."

MORE PROMISES TO THE OVERCOMER

- The promise Christ gives to the overcomers in the church at Laodicea is that He will dine with them. This could refer to the Marriage Supper of the Lamb and the Millennium.
- He also promises that they will sit with Him on His throne. This refers to our reigning with Him on earth.

- We must work for Him because we love Him, but it is encouraging and motivating to know that our rewards lie ahead. They include the Marriage Supper of the Lamb and reigning with Christ forever.

OUR REWARDS

- John, who wrote the Book of Revelation, also wrote that believers should work to receive a full reward (2 John 8).
- It is each believer's personal responsibility and privilege to receive a full reward.
- Paul taught that some Christians will be saved but will not receive a reward (1 Corinthians 3:15) and Jesus taught that there will be degrees of reward.
- David will rule over the whole nation of Israel.
- The 12 Apostles will rule over each of the 12 tribes of Israel.
- Jesus said that some believers would rule over two cities, others would rule over five, and still others would rule over ten cities. Obviously some will be assigned more to rule over than others.
- Paul wrote that some believers' works will be like gold, silver, and precious stones and other believers' works will be like wood, hay, and stubble. Such works will be burned up in the fire of God's judgment (1 Corinthians 3:12-15).
- It will be wonderful to go to heaven and enjoy eternal life, but it will be so disappointing if we don't hear Jesus say, "Well done good and faithful servant."
- Salvation is free but our rewards must be earned by our works of love and service and our lives of obedience.

REVELATION:
CHAPTER FOUR

Starting with this chapter John writes the third division of his vision.

- John wrote what He had seen in chapter 1, the first division of Revelation.
- He describes his vision of Christ the glorified King.
- In chapters 2 and 3, he wrote the second division, about the things which are, the church.
- In the second division, we read Christ's messages to the seven churches and to the entire church age.
- Now we come to the third and final division.
- John is told to write about the things that shall be after these things, or after the church age.

THE FUTURE

- We are projected into the future as John writes about upcoming events, starting with the Rapture.
- Followed by the glories of heaven.
- The rise of Antichrist.
- The seven year tribulation.
- The 21 judgments from an angry God.
- The Battle of Armageddon.
- The return of Christ to establish His worldwide Kingdom on earth.
- The defeat and the destruction of the Antichrist and all of Christ's enemies.
- The binding of the devil for 1,000 years.

- The Great White throne judgment for the devil, the fallen angels and all the unsaved.
- Future eternity.
- The final division will take the rest of the book to complete.

THE SEVEN YEAR TRIBULATION

- Lack of space will not permit a detailed study of the seven year tribulation.
- I will make the following study as brief as possible; I will also attempt to make it simple.
- God's prophetic time clock ticks only when He is dealing with Israel.
- From the cross to the Rapture, God has not been dealing with the Jews as a nation.
- He has been dealing with "whosoever will" in the dispensation of grace.

DANIEL'S SEVENTY WEEKS

- In Daniel 9:24-27, the Bible declares that God will deal with Israel for 490 years.
- Most translations read 70 weeks or 70 weeks of years. This should be translated 70 "sevens" or 490 years.
- The 490 years are divided into three time periods and when you add the first and the second time periods they total 483 years, and that era closed with the crucifixion of Christ.
- This leaves seven years during which God will again deal with Israel.
- Those seven years are the seven years of tribulation.
- Verse 27 in Daniel 9 teaches that the Antichrist will make a covenant of peace for seven years.
- He will break his peace pact in the middle of the seven years.

- The Antichrist will be revealed to the world when he makes his peace pact with Israel.
- The seven years of tribulation will end at the Battle of Armageddon and the Second Coming of Christ to the earth.

THE RAPTURE IN THE BOOK OF REVELATION

- In chapter 4 we are projected into the future at the Rapture of the church.
- We refer to the Rapture as the Rapture of the church but the Rapture will include the resurrection of the saints of the Old Testament and all ages.

PAUL HAD THE REVELATION OF THE RAPTURE

- Paul best describes the Rapture in 1 Thessalonians 4:13-18.
- He states that the Lord Himself will descend from heaven with a shout.
- He will come with the voice of the archangel.
- He will come with the trump of God. Doesn't that sound like Revelation 4:1 when John hears a voice like a trumpet saying, "Come up here"?
- Jesus will come to the clouds.
- The spirits and souls of the dead in Christ in heaven will come with Him.
- While Christ remains in the clouds, the souls and spirits of the righteous will be reunited with their resurrected bodies.
- The dead in Christ will be resurrected first.
- Then we which are alive and remain at the coming of Christ will be caught up, or raptured to meet Christ in the air.
- Together with the resurrected dead, the living believers will return with Christ to heaven to appear before Him at the Judgment Seat to receive their rewards (Romans 14:10).
- Their rewards will depend on their works since their salvation.

- As we have learned, unfortunately some believers will receive no rewards, although they will be saved (1 Corinthians 3:15).
- After the Judgment Seat the saints of all ages will join in the celebration of the Marriage Supper at the close of the seven year tribulation.
- The Bride will be part of the armies of heaven to come back to earth to fight with Christ at the Battle of Armageddon. This is when the Antichrist and his armies will be defeated (chapter 19).
- Depending on their reward, the Bride of Christ will reign with Christ in the Millennium and then forever.

THE RAPTURE IN VERSE ONE

4:1 *After these things I looked, and behold, a door standing open in heaven. And the first voice which I heard was like a trumpet speaking with me, saying, "Come up here, and I will show you things which must take place after this."*

- The word heaven is mentioned 52 times in the Book of Revelation.
- We place the Rapture in chapter 4 verse 1 because this is the one verse where we can best assign the Rapture in the Book of Revelation.
- There are three other Raptures in the Book of Revelation.
- There is the Rapture of the two witnesses in chapter 11. However, before they are raptured they are killed by the Antichrist and their dead bodies lie in the streets of Jerusalem for three and a half days before they are resurrected and raptured. This obviously does not apply to the church.
- The second Rapture is of the manchild in chapter 12. I believe this refers to the 144,000 Jewish evangelists which I will explain when we deal with that chapter.
- Then the tribulation martyrs will be resurrected and raptured at the end of the seven year tribulation (chapter 20:4).

- It is interesting that in the original Greek, chapter 4 verse 1 begins and ends with the same words, "after these things."
- These things must refer to the seven churches and to the church age.
- John is raptured to heaven and the angel promises to show him things which must take place after these things, or after the church age.
- That is why the Rapture has to take place in verse 1.
- John saw a door open in heaven and a voice like a trumpet saying, "Come up here."
- Remember the open door in chapter 3 verse 8 and the promise that the overcomers would escape the world wide tribulation in chapter 3 verse 10?
- The trumpet voice saying, *Come up here* is similar to Paul's writing about the Rapture in 1 Thessalonians 4: 15-17.
- The church and churches are referred to 19 times in the first three chapters, but after the church is raptured in chapter 4 verse 1, it is not once mentioned on earth during the seven year tribulation because the church is in heaven.
- There are several Scriptures to support the fact that the church will not go through the reign of the Antichrist in the seven year tribulation, but space will not allow us to include them in this book.
- Because we place the Rapture in chapter 4 verse 1 and the Antichrist is not revealed until chapter 6 we conclude that the church will not go through the seven year tribulation.

THE RAPTURE IS NEAR

- I believe that the Rapture is the next great event for the believers on God's prophetic calendar.
- Some people believe that the church will go through the seven year tribulation, but I am not looking for Antichrist, I am looking for Jesus Christ.

- Every believer will go through some tribulation and some Christians will suffer much tribulation, but I believe that no overcoming saint of God will go through the future seven year tribulation which will feature the Antichrist.
- It is called the time of Jacob's (Israel's) trouble (Jeremiah 30:7).
- The word Rapture is not found in the Bible, but like the Trinity described in chapter 1, the truth of the Rapture is clearly taught.

WHY CALL IT THE RAPTURE?

- Several hundred years ago, Jerome, a Roman Catholic scholar, translated the New Testament from Greek into Latin.
- He used the verb *rapere*, when he interpreted the words caught up in 1 Thessaalonians 4:17.
- The Latin word *rapere* is the root word that gives us the word Rapture.
- The word in Latin means to seize or to snatch away suddenly.
- Since Jerome's translation, the word Rapture has been commonly used.
- Some call it a translation, or being caught up.
- Frankly, it is not important what you call it so long as you make it!

NO PROPHECY TO BE FULFILLED BEFORE THE RAPTURE

- There are many prophecies to be fulfilled before the Battle of Armageddon and the Second Coming of Christ to earth but no prophecy has to take place before the Rapture.
- At the Rapture, we will have a glorified body like the body of Jesus after His Resurrection.

- Our glorified bodies will not be subject to time, space or material barriers.
- Our bodies will be like the body of Jesus who appeared to His disciples in the Upper Room even though the door was locked.
- We shall appear and disappear at will and yet, like Jesus, who ate fish with His disciples, our bodies will be of flesh and bone but not flesh and blood (Luke 24:29; 1 Cor. 15:50).
- We shall be like Him (1 John 3:2).
- At the Rapture, we shall meet the Lord face to face, together with our loved ones and the saints of all ages. What a day of rejoicing that will be.
- The Rapture is called the Coming of Christ but it is never called the Second Coming of Christ.
- The Second Coming refers to His coming to the earth with His saints, not to the air for His saints.

THE THRONE IN HEAVEN

4:2 Immediately I was in the Spirit; and behold, a throne set in heaven, and One sat on the throne.
- John was taken to heaven and was inspired by the Spirit to write of the glories of God's throne in heaven and God who was sitting on the throne.
- As we stated earlier, the throne is mentioned over 40 times in the Book of Revelation and is the focus of all heaven's glory and activity.

A DESCRIPTION OF GOD

4:3 And He who sat there was like a jasper and a sardius stone in appearance; and there was a rainbow around the throne, in appearance like an emerald.

74

- The description of God who sits on the throne is difficult for our finite minds to grasp.
- One writer stated that one stone is red, representing the blood and the other is purple, representing royalty.
- They are also the first and last colors of a prism.
- The red sardius stone was the first stone and the jasper was the 12th stone on the priest's breastplate.
- Jasper is transparent.
- We can only wonder what John's reaction was as he saw the eternal God sitting on His throne in heaven.

THE RAINBOW AROUND THE THRONE

- It is reassuring to know that there was a rainbow around the throne of God.
- The rainbow was a sign of God's promise to Noah that He would never again destroy the world with a flood.
- Now in the midst of God's judgments, He displays a rainbow of grace and promise around His throne.

THE TWENTY FOUR ELDERS ARE THE BRIDE OF CHRIST

4:4 Around the throne were twenty-four thrones, and on the thrones I saw twenty-four elders sitting, clothed in white robes; and they had crowns of gold on their heads.
- I believe that the 24 thrones and the 24 elders sitting on the thrones around the throne of God symbolize the Bride of Christ.
- The number 24 represents the 12 Old Testament tribes of Israel and the 12 New Testament Apostles of the church.
- This is confirmed in Revelation chapter 21 verses 12 through 15.

- The Bible states that the 12 names on the gates and the 12 names on the foundations of the New Jerusalem (totaling 24) represent the Bride of Christ.
- The word "elders" is a name used by both Israel and by the church.
- The fact that the elders are wearing crowns suggests that this event is after the Judgment Seat of Christ when we will receive crowns to symbolize our position and place of authority as we reign with Him in His coming Kingdom for 1,000 years and then forever.
- Some teach that the 24 elders are angels, but angels are never seen in Revelation wearing crowns and sitting on thrones.
- In the Bible elders are always men, not angels.
- The Bible teaches that redeemed men and women, not angels will reign with Christ.

ACTIVITIES AROUND THE THRONE

4:5 And from the throne proceeded lightnings, thunderings, and voices. Seven lamps of fire were burning before the throne, which are the seven Spirits of God.
6a Before the throne there was a sea of glass, like crystal.
- The throne of God is located in a temple in heaven (chapter 15:5).
- From the throne of God comes thunder, lightening and voices.
- This speaks of judgment.
- There are seven lamps of fire representing the seven Spirits of God.
- This again teaches the completeness and the perfection of the one Holy Spirit.
- There is a sea of glass like crystal before the throne.
- The sea of glass depicts a calm sea without restless storms.
- Peace and eternal rest are what we have to look forward to.

- In this chapter the sea of glass is unoccupied but in chapter 15 there is a great multitude standing on the sea of glass.

THE FOUR LIVING CREATURES

4:6b And in the midst of the throne, and around the throne were four living creatures full of eyes in front and in back.
7 The first living creature was like a lion, the second living creature like a calf (an ox), the third living creature had a face like a man, and the fourth living creature was like a flying eagle.
8 The four living creatures, each having six wings, were full of eyes around and within. And they do not rest day or night, saying: "Holy, holy, holy, Lord God Almighty, Who was and is and is to come!"
9 Whenever the living creatures give glory and honor and thanks to Him who sits on the throne who lives for ever and ever,

- John sees four living creatures, or, four unique angelic beings.
- Each had a different face.
- The first had the face of a man.
- The second had the face of an eagle.
- The third had the face of an ox.
- The fourth had the face of a lion.

THEIR FOUR FACES REPRESENT CHRIST

- They represent the four characteristics of Christ revealed in the Gospels.
- Matthew depicts Christ as the King of the Jews—the face of a lion.
- Mark portrays Christ as the Servant—the face of the ox.
- Luke presents Christ as the Son of Man—the face of the man.

- John introduces Jesus as the Son of God—the face of the eagle, the king of the heavenly birds. The eagle can soar higher in the heavens than any other bird.

A DESCRIPTION OF THE LIVING CREATURES

- These angelic creatures each had six wings.
- They had eyes around and within.
- This means that they see everything clearly and accurately.
- They may be the same angels that Isaiah saw in Isaiah chapter 6.
- They continually say, Holy, Holy, Holy, an expression of worship for each member of the Godhead.
- They also revealed to John the mysteries of the seven seals—(chapter 6).

THE LIVING CREATURES PERFORM SEVEN ACTS OF MINISTRY

1. They call attention to God's holiness.
2. They fall prostrate before God in worship.
3. They sing, worship and play harps.
4. They offer up the prayers of the saints to God (chapter 5: 8-10).
5. They call forth the 4 horsemen of the Apocalypse (chapter 6:1-8).
6. They give the seven bowls of judgment to the seven angels who will pour them out on the earth (chapter 15:7).
7. They listen to the worship of others (chapter 14:3).

THE TWENTY FOUR ELDERS WORSHIP

4:10 the twenty-four elders fall down before Him who sits on the throne and worship Him who lives forever and ever,

and cast their crowns before the throne, saying:
4:11 "You are worthy, O Lord, to receive glory and honor and
  power; For You created all things, And by Your will they
  exist and were created" (the KJV says "for your pleasure").
- Worship is contagious.
- The 24 elders join the angels. What an anthem!
- All the angels of heaven and all the redeemed of earth are
  singing praise to our God before His throne.
- As we sing we will cast our crowns before Him.
- Verse 11 tells us part of the song we will sing.
- Verse 11 also describes the purpose of creation.

THE TWENTY FOUR ELDERS PERFORM THE FOLLOWING MINISTRY

- They sit on thrones.
- They worship God.
- They wear white robes.
- They wear crowns.
- They cast their crowns before God.
- They fall prostrate in worship before God.
- They sing.
- They play harps as do the angels (chapter 5:8-10).
- They act as priests (chapter 5:8).
- They help John to understand the vision (chapters 5:5; 7:13-14).

MORE FUTURE EVENTS

- The following chapters present more of the glories of
  heaven—and more revelation of the Lord Jesus Christ.
- Chapters 6-19 also describe the activities of the Antichrist.

REVELATION:
CHAPTER FIVE

This chapter presents Christ as the Worthy Lamb who becomes the Lion of the Tribe of Judah.

SEALS, TRUMPETS, AND BOWLS OF JUDGMENT

- The seven seals of judgment and the seven trumpets of judgment occur in the first half of the tribulation.
- This is called the lesser tribulation because the Antichrist will be protecting Israel because of his peace pact.
- The seven bowls of judgment occur in the second half of the seven year tribulation.
- This is called the great tribulation because the Antichrist will try to destroy the Jewish nation completely.
- Each judgment occurs in consecutive order.
- They become more severe as they happen.
- They climax with the Battle of Armageddon and the Second Coming of Christ.
- The Book of Revelation speaks of 42 months (or three and a half years); 1,260 days (or three and a half years). And both Revelation and Daniel speak of "a time"—that is 1; and "times"—that is 2, making 3. And "half a time"—which totals 3 and a half times (or 3 three and a half years).
- This refers to the last half of the tribulation.

SEVEN SEALS OF JUDGMENTS

- First seal   — Antichrist.
- Second Seal   — War.
- Third Seal   — Hunger and Famine.
- Fourth Seal   — Pestilence and Death.
- Fifth Seal   — Martyrdom.
- Sixth Seal   — Cosmic Happenings in heaven and earth.
- Seventh Seal — Silence in heaven.

The seven seals of judgment begin in chapter six, but they are introduced in this chapter.

THE LAMB TAKES THE SEVEN SEALED SCROLL

5:1 And I saw in the right hand of Him who sat on the throne a scroll written inside and on the back, sealed with seven seals.

2 Then I saw a strong angel proclaiming with a loud voice, "Who is worthy to open the scroll and to loose its seals?"

- In the Roman Empire in John's day, it was the custom for the will of a wealthy person to be written on a scroll and sealed with seals.
- These seals were usually the signet rings of seven witnesses.
- In order for the will to be opened, the unsealing had to be done in the presence of a judge.
- There were also elders present for the reading of the will.
- John saw a will written on a scroll, which had been legally sealed and was in the right hand of Almighty God.
- The right hand always speaks of power, blessing and authority.
- The Bible does not explain the contents of the book, but the seals had to be broken for the contents to be revealed.
- Some scholars teach that the contents contained the message of redemption, but redemption had already been purchased.

- Others teach that the scroll contained the title deed to the earth, but the earth already belongs to the Lord.
- I believe that the contents are the seven seals of judgment outlined above.

ANGELS IN HEAVEN

- The Book of Revelation mentions an angel with a loud voice 13 times.
- Many times the angels in Revelation are identified, but 26 angels are not identified and one of the unidentified angels is mentioned in this verse.

NO ONE WAS WORTHY TO OPEN THE SCROLL

5:3 And no one in heaven or on the earth or under the earth was able to open the scroll, or to look at it.
4 So I wept much, because no one was found worthy to open and read the scroll, or to look at it.
- John wept uncontrollably because no one was worthy to open the scroll, or to read or even to look at the scroll.

THE LAMB BECOMES THE LION

5:5 But one of the elders said to me, "Do not weep. Behold, the Lion of the tribe of Judah, the Root of David, has prevailed to open the scroll and to loose its seven seals."
6 And I looked, and behold, in the midst of the throne and of the four living creatures, and in the midst of the elders, stood a Lamb as though it had been slain, having seven horns and seven eyes, which are the seven Spirits of God sent out into all the earth.
- Jesus Christ has several titles in the book of Revelation, but in verse 5, He is called, the Lion of the tribe of Judah.

• Judah was the leading tribe in Israel and the lion is the king of the beasts.
• The kings of Israel came from the tribe of Judah.
• Thus, Jesus Christ is King of kings.
• He is also called the Root of David.
• This means that Christ's victory has given Him the authority to rule as King on the throne of His father David for all eternity.
• He is also called the slain Lamb (verse 6).
• Jesus won the victory and is now the Lion King because He was willing to suffer as the slain Lamb.
• The word slain in the Greek means a violent death.
• The word Lamb is mentioned 27 times in the Book of Revelation and yet Paul never used the word Lamb in his writings and Peter used it only once in his epistles.

REDEMPTION BY THE BLOOD OF THE LAMB

• Redemption by the blood of a lamb has been taught throughout the Bible:
• The blood of a lamb brought salvation to a man, Abel.
• The blood of a lamb brought salvation to a family on the night of the Passover, in Egypt.
• The blood of a lamb brought salvation to a nation, the nation of Israel each year on the Day of Atonement.
• John the Baptist introduced Jesus as the Lamb of God who takes away, not the sins of a man; not the sins of a family; not the sins of a nation, but, thank God, Jesus is the Lamb of God who takes away the sins of the whole world.
• The cleansing blood of a Lamb began as a small spring in Genesis; it become a stream and a river in Exodus, but at Calvary, it became a raging torrent of Divine blessing, mercy, grace and power.

THE SEVEN HORNS

- They symbolized the totality of the power and authority of the Holy Spirit's anointing that rests upon King Jesus.
- The number seven also suggests that Christ has absolute, world wide power.

THE SEVEN EYES

- They symbolize the seven Spirits of God.
- As we have learned earlier, the number seven symbolizes the totality, the perfection, the completeness of the knowledge and wisdom of the Holy Spirit.
- It could also suggest that Christ sees all and knows all that is happening in the seven continents and the whole world.

WORTHY IS THE LAMB

5:7 Then He came and took the scroll out of the right hand of Him who sat on the throne. Worthy Is the Lamb
- The Lamb took the scroll from the right hand of the Father.
- Christ alone is worthy.

5:8 Now when He had taken the scroll, the four living creatures and the twenty-four elders fell down before the Lamb, each having a harp, and golden bowls full of incense, which are the prayers of the saints.
- Throughout the Book of Revelation heaven is filled with volumes of vocal praise and worship accompanied by musical instruments.
- Jesus is worthy of our praise.
- In verse 8, prayer is mingled with praise.

5:9 And they sang a new song, saying: "You are worthy to take the scroll, And to open its seals; For You were slain, And have redeemed us (them) to God by Your blood Out of every tribe and tongue and people and nation,
10 And have made us (them) kings and priests to our God; And we shall reign on the earth."

- The word, "us" in verses 9 and 10 should be translated, "them"— referring to the saints mentioned in verse 8.
- The reason is because the 4 angelic living creatures were not redeemed by the blood of the Lamb.
- This translation is confirmed by all the prominent Greek scholars I have researched who have written commentaries on the Book of Revelation.

HEAVEN'S ANTHEM

5:11 Then I looked, and I heard the voice of many angels around the throne, the living creatures, and the elders; and the number of them was ten thousand times ten thousand, and thousands of thousands,

- As Jesus the Lamb took the scroll out of the Father's right hand there was an innumerable multitude who made up the heavenly choir and the heavenly musicians.
- Some Christians teach that it is a sin to have instruments in the church, but if instruments are in heaven, why not on earth?
- The object of praise and worship is the Lamb that was slain.
- The reason for our praise and worship is that we have been redeemed by the precious blood of the Lamb and He has made us kings and priests to our God.
- When we return to earth with King Jesus, we shall reign with Him as kings on the earth for one thousand years and then forever.

5:12 saying with a loud voice: "Worthy is the Lamb who was slain to receive power and riches and wisdom, and strength and honor and glory and blessing!"

- The Lamb is worthy to be praised:
- The word "worship" comes from an old English word, Worthship.
- Jesus is worshiped because He is worthy.

ALL CREATION WORSHIPS

5:13 And every creature which is in heaven and on the earth and under the earth and such as are in the sea, and all that are in them, I heard saying: " Blessing and honor and glory and power Be to Him who sits on the throne, And to the Lamb, for forever and ever!"

- Worship is given to the Lamb by the angels, the living creatures and the 24 elders who represent the saints in heaven.
- An anthem of praise and worship came from an innumerable multitude.
- They sang of power, riches, wisdom, strength, honor, glory and blessing.

THE CONCLUSION OF PRAISE AND WORSHIP

5:14 Then the four living creatures said, "Amen!" And the twenty-four elders fell down and worshiped Him who lives forever and ever.

- This verse concludes the anthem of praise from the angels and all of the redeemed.
- However, there is much more praise and worship in the remaining chapters.

Revelation:
Chapter Six

Now we come to the amazing events which will unveil the Antichrist and unleash the Battle of Armageddon.

The Final Seven Years of History Before Jesus Returns

- We are now entering the period of time called the seven year Tribulation.
- This will be the final seven years of history before Jesus returns to earth to fight at the Battle of Armageddon and to establish His world wide Kingdom.
- As we have already learned, the tribulation is divided into two periods of three and a half years.
- We have also learned that the seven seals of judgment and the seven trumpets of judgment occur in the first half of the seven years and the seven bowls of judgment occur in the final three and a half years.
- The seven seals of judgment were listed in order in chapter 5. Now we examine each seal in detail.

The Four Horsemen of the Apocalypse

6:1 Now I saw when the Lamb opened one of the seals; and I heard one of the four living creatures saying with a voice like thunder, "Come and see."

- As Jesus, the Lamb, opens each of the seven seals on the scroll, each of the seven judgments is revealed.
- As the seals are opened, each of the four angelic living creatures says to John, "Come and see."
- Ten times in the Book of Revelation John records that he hears the sound of thunder in heaven. This is a sign of judgment.

The First Seal Introduces the Antichrist

6:2 *And I looked, and behold, a white horse. He who sat on it had a bow; and a crown was given to him, and he went out conquering and to conquer.*

- Christ takes the seven sealed scroll out of the Father's right hand and breaks each of them one at a time.
- As each seal is broken, the contents of the seal are revealed.
- The first seal introduces a white horse rider.
- Some teach that the rider on the white horse is Jesus because He will return to earth riding on a white horse in chapter 19.
- There are obvious distinctions between the two riders.
- This rider carries a bow but Jesus carries a sword.
- This rider brings war, famine, pestilence and death but Jesus returns to establish His Kingdom of peace, blessing and prosperity.
- This rider is symbolic but Jesus will come literally.
- This rider is on earth but Jesus will come from heaven to earth.
- The rider cannot be Christ because He is the One opening the seals.
- Another theory is that the white horse rider symbolizes the preaching of the Gospel.
- I believe that the white horse rider is the Antichrist.
- The Bible refers to the spirit of Antichrist; many Antichrists and this personality called the Antichrist, or the Man of Sin.
- The Antichrist will dominate the last seven years before Jesus returns to earth to rule as King of kings and Lord of lords.
- His name can mean "against Christ" or "another Christ."

THE TEN NATION CONFEDERATION IN REVISED ROME

- Daniel 7 teaches that the Antichrist will come from one of ten nations after they have formed as an international confederation within the boundary of the former Roman Empire.
- Whether this union of confederate nations will form before or after the Rapture, the Bible does not say.
- Nor does the Bible tell us how long it will have existed before the Antichrist is revealed.
- It does state that it will be a confederation of ten nations before the Antichrist is revealed because he comes out of 1 of them after they are formed.
- The Antichrist will introduce himself as a man of peace and will make a seven year peace treaty with Israel. That is why he has a bow with no arrows.
- However, the Bible states that he will quickly become a man of war and he will attack and defeat three of the ten nations and the other nations will submit to him.
- In the middle of the seven year tribulation he will be ruling over all ten nations; he will break his peace pact with Israel; he will invade the land of Israel and will try to annihilate the Jews.
- This will be the beginning of the Battle of Armageddon.
- The Antichrist will lead the most powerful military alliance in human history.
- Demon spirits will also empower his words and words spoken by the dragon and the False Prophet.
- They will influence many other nations to submit to the leadership of the Antichrist and be influenced by his hatred for and hostility to the nation of Israel.

WARS IN THE MIDDLE EAST

- Before the Battle of Armageddon, there will be continuous wars fought in the Middle East.

- The battles will be fought over Israel. Some wars will also be fought even before the Antichrist is revealed.
- These wars will prepare the way for the Antichrist's peace treaty with Israel.
- God has staked His eternal reputation over the survival of Israel.
- This is why Satan hates the Jews and the land of Israel.
- No one will bring peace to the Middle East until the Antichrist makes a seven year treaty which will guarantee peace in Israel.
- As we have also learned, he will break the peace treaty after three and a half years and Satan will give him power to try and destroy Israel at the Battle of Armageddon.

THE ANTICHRIST AND HIS DESTRUCTION

- A few years ago, Henry Spaak, a spokesman for the Common Market in Brussels, said, "Send us a man and be he God or devil, we will accept him." He probably did not know that his words were prophetic.
- The Antichrist will be controlled by Satan.
- However, as we have learned he will be defeated by Christ the King because when the Antichrist has surrounded Israel and their allies at the Battle of Armageddon, the Jews will pray for their Messiah to return and deliver them from the military power of the Antichrist.
- Jesus will return, Israel will be delivered and the enemies of Israel will be destroyed.
- Christ will establish His worldwide Kingdom on earth.
- The devil and his agents will be bound for 1,000 years (chapter 20:1-3).

NEBUCHADNEZZAR'S DREAM

- In Daniel chapter 2, the Bible describes Nebuchadnezzar's dream.

- He dreamed of an image with a head of gold, symbolizing the Empire of Babylon.
- The chest and two arms of silver, symbolizing the Medes and Persians which conquered the Babylonian Empire.
- The thighs of brass, symbolizing the succeeding world power, the Empire of Greece under Alexander the Great.
- The two legs of iron, symbolizing the eastern and western divisions of the old Roman Empire. The Roman Empire was in power during John's day.
- The two feet and ten toes of iron and clay, which Daniel explained to be the ten nation confederation which will be formed in the last days within the boundary of the former Roman Empire.
- The ten nations will be ten sovereign nations, each with their own king (leader) and after they have joined together, the Antichrist will come from one of them.
- As we have learned, he will declare war on three of them and by the middle of the seven year tribulation he will be ruling over all of the ten nations to establish the eighth and final world power.
- This final world power will be defeated and destroyed at the Battle of Armageddon at the Second Coming of Christ.

THE TEN NATIONS WILL NOT ALL COME FROM EUROPE

- Today, it is commonly taught by several well known prophecy preachers that the ten nation confederation will all come from Europe.
- I cannot accept this teaching because, Daniel teaches that the ten toes represent the ten nations of the Antichrist's kingdom.
- Obviously, the image did not have ten toes on one foot so it is only logical to conclude that five nations will come from one leg, the eastern division of the former Roman Empire, the

Middle East and five nations will come from the other leg, the western division of the former Roman Empire, Europe.
- Thus, there will be a confederation of five European nations and five Middle Eastern nations.
- These ten nations are symbolized not only by the ten toes of Daniel 2, but by the ten horns of Daniel 7; Revelation 13; and Revelation 17.

THE ANTICHRIST WILL COME FROM THE MIDDLE EAST

- I believe that the Antichrist will come from the Middle East because, he is called, "The king of Babylon" (Isaiah 14:4).
- He is called, "The Assyrian" (Isaiah 10:20-27). The ancient Assyrian Empire was made up of Middle Eastern nations.
- He is called, "The king of the north" (Daniel 11:36-45).
- Some prophecy preachers have wrongly concluded that this teaches that the Antichrist comes from Russia, but Russia was never part of the old Roman Empire.
- The north refers to the northern division of two nations of the former Grecian Empire, namely Egypt and Syria.
- Thus, the northern nation from which the Antichrist will come will be Syria (Daniel 8 and Daniel 11).

THE SECOND SEAL BRINGS WAR

6:3 When He opened the second seal, I heard the second living creature saying, "Come and see."
4 Another horse, fiery red, went out. And it was granted to the one who sat on it to take peace from the earth, and that people should kill one another; and there was given to him a great sword.
- During the seven year tribulation, the Antichrist and the other of the four horsemen of the Apocalypse are revealed as satanic personalities.

- The second seal of judgment brings war on the earth.

THE THIRD SEAL BRINGS INFLATION AND FAMINE

6:5 When He opened the third seal, I heard the third living creature say, "Come and see." So I looked, and behold, a black horse, and he who sat on it had a pair of scales in his hand.

- The black horse rider carries a pair of scales symbolizing famine.
- As I write this book, Congress has just passed the giant multi billion dollar Wall Street bail out.
- With the additional spending plus the budget deficit, the figure has reached into the trillions of dollars.
- The Bible prophesies that during the seven year tribulation, inflation, famine and hunger will be wide spread.
- According to chapter 18, even gold, silver, and precious stones will ultimately be worthless.
- The following statistics on world hunger are beyond belief.
- More than 800,000,000 will go to bed hungry tonight and every night on our planet.
- 25,000 people die of starvation every day.
- At least 50 people will die of starvation before you finish reading this page.
- 2,000,000 babies die every year because of malnutrition.
- 225,000,000 children worldwide have physical and mental problems due to malnutrition.
- In America, the richest nation in the world, 33,000,000 go to bed hungry; that is one out of every six people in the nation.
- In a nation close to America's shores, many poor, pathetic and hungry people are eating dirt in a desperate effort to survive.
- More than 1 billion people on the planet earn less than $1 a day.
- When the Antichrist is revealed conditions will get worse.
- In the Antichrist's kingdom together with other nations under his diabolical control, no one will be able to buy or sell

unless they have the mark of the beast or 666, the number of his name.

- This means that business, commerce and trading will be totally controlled by the Antichrist.

A DAY'S WAGES TO SURVIVE

6:6 And I heard a voice in the midst of the four living creatures saying, "A quart of wheat for a denarius, and three quarts of barley for a denarius; and do not harm the oil and the wine."

- A denarius was a slave's daily ration.
- Food will be much more expensive to buy in the tribulation.

THE FOURTH SEAL BRINGS PESTILENCE AND DEATH

6:7 When He opened the fourth seal, I heard the voice of the fourth living creature saying, "Come and see."
8 So I looked, and behold, a pale horse. And the name of him who sat on it was Death, and Hades followed with him. And power was given to them over a fourth of the earth, to kill with sword, with hunger, with death, and by the beasts of the earth.

- The Antichrist is symbolized by the white horse rider.
- War is symbolized by the red horse rider.
- War brings hunger and famine, symbolized by the black horse rider.
- Hunger and famine bring pestilence and death, symbolized by the pale horse riders.
- The result of these judgments is that a quarter of the world's population will die and this is only the beginning of the seven years of tribulation. It gets worse, much worse.
- The word pale is better translated a pale yellowish green.

- In ancient Greek literature, this color was used to describe the color of a corpse.
- The beasts of the earth may mean that hungry wild animals will invade our population centers and actually attack and consume human beings for food.
- Or it could refer to pestilences and diseases caught from animals such as mad cow disease and aids which many scientists believe came from the green monkey virus.

THE FIFTH SEAL INTRODUCES MARTYRS

6:9 When He opened the fifth seal, I saw under the altar the souls of those who had been slain for the word of God and for the testimony which they held.
10 And they cried with a loud voice, saying, "How long, O Lord, holy and true, until you judge and avenge our blood on those who dwell on the earth?"
11 Then a white robe was given to each of them; and it was said to them that they should rest a little while longer, until both the number of their fellow servants and their brethren, who would be killed as they were, was completed.

- The fifth seal introduces us to the first group of many martyrs who will be killed in the seven year tribulation.
- These verses give lie to those who teach soul sleep.
- Soul sleep means that at death there is no consciousness until the resurrection.
- The above verses teach that the souls of these tribulation martyrs are fully conscious in heaven.
- The martyrs remember what happened to them when they were killed on the earth.
- They are having a conversation with Jesus and want to know when He is going to judge the people who killed them.

- Jesus replies that there are other people who will also be martyred for their faith in the seven year tribulation and when the last one has been killed, He will judge their enemies.
- All the tribulation martyrs will be resurrected and raptured to heaven in one group at the end of the seven year tribulation in time to celebrate the Marriage Supper of the Lamb.
- Their souls are under the altar. In the Old Testament the altar was always a place of blood sacrifice.
- Even though they get to heaven by dying the death of a martyr, their redemption is assured because Jesus shed His blood.

THE RESURRECTION AND THE FEAST OF FIRSTFRUITS

- There will be many people saved during the seven year tribulation.
- Unfortunately, apart from the 144,000 Jewish evangelists described in chapters 7 and 14, no one will get to heaven without experiencing martyrdom.
- To fully understand why people will be saved after the Rapture, I will illustrate with the Old Testament Feast of First Fruits.
- At harvest time, the priest would present one sheaf and wave that sheaf before the Lord.
- Then the workers would gather the main harvest.
- Finally they would gather the gleanings.
- The gleanings were the part of the harvest that had been left behind when the main harvest was gathered.
- Some of the gleanings had been trodden down and trampled under foot, but were reaped after the main harvest had been gathered.
- The harvest was not complete until the gleanings had been gathered.

THE MEANING OF THE HARVEST

- The Bible declares that Christ is the first fruits of the resurrection (1 Corinthians 15:20).
- The Rapture and the resurrection illustrate the main harvest.
- The people who will be saved during the tribulation illustrate the gleanings.
- They were left behind at the Rapture but were saved in the tribulation by dying as a martyr.
- The harvest of the resurrection of the righteous dead and the Rapture of the living believers will not be complete without the gleanings (the martyrs).

THE SIXTH SEAL BRINGS COSMIC DISTURBANCES

6:12 I looked when He opened the sixth seal, and behold, there was a great earthquake; and the sun became black as sackcloth of hair, and the moon became like blood.

13 And the stars of heaven fell to the earth, as a fig tree drops its late figs when it is shaken by a mighty wind.

14 Then the sky receded as a scroll when it is rolled up, and every mountain and island was moved out of its place.

15 And the kings of the earth, the great men, the rich men, the commanders, the mighty men, every slave and every free man, hid themselves in the caves and in the rocks of the mountains,

16 and said to the mountains and rocks, "Fall on us and hide us from the face of Him who sits on the throne and from the wrath of the Lamb!

17 For the great day of His wrath has come, and who is able to stand?"

- Cosmic disturbances will occur in the sixth seal of judgment.
- The first of four earthquakes will occur during the sixth seal in the seven year tribulation.

- These earthquakes will shake the major cities of the world.
- Jesus also predicted earthquakes in the last days.
- The sun became black.
- This was also predicted by the prophet Joel and by Jesus as an event of the last days.
- Five times during the seven year tribulation, the sun will be darkened.
- There was a dark day recorded in New England on May 19, 1880, but that was nothing in comparison to what will happen during the sixth seal of judgment.
- The moon became like blood.
- This will also happen five times during the seven year tribulation.
- This was also prophesied by Joel and by Jesus as a last day event.
- Stars fell from heaven.
- Corresponding to the sun and moon being affected, the Book of Revelation states five different times that the stars will be affected, but only twice in the book do we read that stars actually fall from heaven.
- This will happen here and during the sixth bowl of judgment at the end of the seven year tribulation when Jesus returns.
- Some scholars believe this refers to meteors.
- This also was prophesied as a last day event by Joel and by Jesus.

THE HEAVENS WILL SHAKE

- John records that the heavens will recede like a scroll.
- In Matthew 24, Jesus also prophesied that the powers of the heavens will be shaken.
- The Book of Revelation teaches that there will be a new heaven and a new earth for all eternity.
- This means that the results of sin in the universe will be renovated by fire.

- The Bible teaches that the heavens and the earth are eternal but they will be made new.
- Mountains and islands will be moved.
- This could be caused by the earthquake.
- It does not mean that mountains and islands will cease to exist because they are mentioned several other times later in the Book of Revelation.
- In that day, men will cry to the mountains and hills to fall on them to hide them from God's judgment and from the wrath of the Lamb because the great day of God's anger has arrived.
- Jesus also stated that in the last days, *Men's heart will fail them for fear...looking after those things which are coming on the earth* (Luke 21:26).

MATTHEW TWENTY FOUR AND REVELATION SIX COMPARED

It is interesting to compare the similarities of the prophecies of Jesus recorded in Matthew 24 and the first six seals of judgment recorded in Revelation chapter 6:

- Antichrist   - Matthew 24:5   Revelation 6:2.
- War   - Matthew 24:6-8   Revelation 6:3-4.
- Famine   - Matthew 24:4-7   Revelation 6:5-6.
- Death   - Matthew 24:7-9   Revelation 5:7-8.
- Martyrdom   - Matthew 24:9-10   Revelation 6:9-10.
- Cosmic changes   - Matthew 24:29   Revelation 6:12-17.

OTHER PROPHECIES CONFIRM REVELATION'S PROPHECIES

- Several Old Testament prophets who lived hundreds of years before Jesus and John also predicted these same judgments accurately.

- God's Word is infallible and true.
- Man can find no contradictions in its pages because they are inspired by the Holy Spirit.

The Wrath of God and the Lamb

- The breaking of the seals introduces the wrath of the Lamb.
- The wrath of God will be poured out in the last three and a half years of the future seven year tribulation.
- The exact meaning of the word wrath is extreme or fiery anger.
- Today is the dispensation of grace, but after the Rapture will be the time for judgment.

REVELATION:
CHAPTER SEVEN

This is a parenthetical chapter of both grace and judgment. Many scholars try to explain why the tribe of Manasah replaces the tribe of Dan, but if John did not explain, why should we speculate?

THE 144,000 JEWISH EVANGELISTS

- The Jehovah's Witnesses teach that only 144,000 of their cult will go to heaven and the quota has already been filled.
- Other groups teach that the 144,000 are the Seventh Day Adventists.
- Still others claim that the 144,000 are the forerunners of the Anglo Saxon race.
- The Bible teaches that the 144,000 will all be Jewish—missionary-evangelists.

CHRIST HAS ALWAYS HAD
A WITNESS ON THE EARTH

- Since Jesus ascended back to heaven, the church has been His witness on the earth (Acts 1:8).
- After the Rapture, the 144,000 Jewish missionaries will become His witnesses.
- After their ministry they will be raptured and the two witnesses will be Christ's representatives.

THE 144,000 PROTECTED

7:1 After these things I saw four angels standing at the four corners of the earth, holding the four winds of the earth, that the wind should not blow on the earth, on the sea, or on any tree.
- Some years ago I read in the Readers' Digest that scientists have discovered the four corners of the earth.
- The four winds are also mentioned in Daniel 7:2 and Daniel 8:8.
- Jesus also talked about the four winds of heaven (Matthew 24:31).

THE SEVEN ANGELS BLOWING SEVEN TRUMPETS

7:2 Then I saw another angel ascending from the east, having the seal of the living God. And he cried with a loud voice to the four angels to whom it was granted to harm the earth and the sea,
- These are the first four of the seven angels who will blow the trumpets which will release even greater judgments upon the earth.

7:3 saying, "Do not harm the earth, the sea, or the trees till we have sealed the servants of our God on their foreheads."
4 And I heard the number of those who were sealed. One hundred and forty-four thousand of all the tribes of the children of Israel were sealed:
- Before the Lamb opens the seventh seal and the seven angels blow the seven trumpets of judgment, God reveals His grace by commissioning 144,000 Jewish evangelists to preach the gospel to the whole world.
- God holds back His judgment until these witnesses have received His seal of protection.

- Just as many ungodly people will receive the Mark of the Beast as the Antichrist's seal or they will receive 666 the number of the Antichrist in their right hands or in their foreheads, so the 144,000 Jewish evangelists will be sealed with God's seal in their foreheads to protect them from coming judgment.

THE 144,000 IDENTIFIED

7:5 of the tribe of Judah twelve thousand were sealed; of the tribe of Reuben twelve thousand were sealed; of the tribe of Gad twelve thousand were sealed;
6 of the tribe of Asher twelve thousand were sealed; of the tribe of Naphtali twelve thousand were sealed; of the tribe of Manasseh twelve thousand were sealed;
7 of the tribe of Simeon twelve thousand were sealed; of the tribe of Levi twelve thousand were sealed; of the tribe of Issachar twelve thousand were sealed;
8 of the tribe of Zebulun twelve thousand were sealed; of the tribe of Joseph twelve thousand were sealed; of the tribe of Benjamin twelve thousand were sealed.
- The 144,000 are all Jewish evangelists.
- 12,000 come from 12 tribes totaling 144,000.
- The name of each tribe is mentioned.

THEY ARE SEALED

- Sealing is the work of the Holy Spirit.
- Not only will the 144,000 Jewish missionary evangelists be sealed by the Holy Spirit to protect them from the seven trumpet judgments, they will also be sealed by the Holy Spirit to anoint them for their ministry.

The Holy Spirit Works in the Tribulation

- As a boy growing up in a traditional Pentecostal church I heard many preachers say that when the Rapture took place, the Holy Spirit would be removed from the earth.
- This is false because the Holy Spirit will be very active during the seven year tribulation.
- He will seal and anoint the 144,000 Jewish missionary evangelists.
- Verse 9 below teaches that multitudes will be saved.
- No one can be saved apart from the ministry of the Holy Spirit.
- As we learned earlier, the Jehovah's Witnesses teach that only 144,000 of their group will go to heaven, but in these verses, the Bible teaches that multitudes will be saved and will go to heaven.
- The Bible states that they washed their robes in the blood of the Lamb. This is possible only by the ministry of the Holy Spirit.
- The two witnesses will be killed, resurrected and raptured. The Bible says that their resurrection will be the work of the Holy Spirit.
- The 144,000 are on earth in chapter 7 and in heaven in chapter 14.
- Their rapture will be the ministry of the Holy Spirit.
- At the end of the tribulation the Jews will have a special outpouring of the Holy Spirit (Zechariah 12:10 and Joel 2 and 3).
- The tribulation martyrs will be resurrected and raptured at the end of the seven year tribulation. This will be the ministry of the Holy Spirit.

A Great Multitude in Heaven

7:9 After these things I looked, and behold, a great multitude which no one could number, of all nations, tribes, peoples, and tongues, standing before the throne and before the Lamb, clothed with white robes, with palm branches in their hands,

- After John saw the vision of the 144,000 Jewish evangelists, he sees a group of saints in heaven who had been martyred for their faith.
- He describes them as a great multitude standing before the throne of God and before the Lamb.
- They are clothed with white robes of righteousness and have palm branches in their hands.
- Palm branches were used as a symbol of victory and Palms were used in the Feast of Tabernacles.

WORSHIP IN HEAVEN

7:10 and crying out with a loud voice, saying, "Salvation belongs to our God who sits on the throne, and to the Lamb!"

11 All the angels stood around the throne and the elders and the four living creatures, and fell on their faces before the throne and worshiped God,

12 saying: "Amen! Blessing and glory and wisdom, Thanksgiving and honor and power and might, Be to our God forever and ever. Amen."

- Because of the multitudes who were saved everyone in heaven begins to worship God the Father and the Lamb.
- Their worship consists of an Amen at the beginning and an Amen at the end.
- Between the two Amen they sing praises of blessing, glory, wisdom, thanksgiving, honor, power, and might be to our God forever.
- All the praise and worship in heaven is centered in the person of God, while much of what we call praise and worship on earth is centered in man.

The 144,000 Came
out of Great Tribulation

7:13 Then one of the elders answered, saying to me, "Who are these arrayed in white robes, and where did they come from?"

14 And I said to him, "Sir, you know." So he said to me, "These are the ones who come out of the great tribulation, and washed their robes and made them white in the blood of the Lamb.

- These people did not make the Rapture.
- One of the elders said that they had come out of great tribulation, which is the final half of the tribulation.
- They were martyrs who were killed because they refused to take the mark of the beast or 666, the number of the Antichrist's name.
- They had washed their robes and made them white in the blood of the Lamb.
- Thus, they were part of the blood washed redeemed, but were saved and martyred after the Rapture.

No More Tribulation

7:15 Therefore they are before the throne of God, and serve Him day and night in His temple. And He who sits on the throne will dwell among them.

16 They shall neither hunger anymore nor thirst anymore; the sun shall not strike them, nor any heat;

17 for the Lamb who is in the midst of the throne will shepherd them and lead them to living fountains of waters. And God will wipe away every tear from their eyes.

- These martyrs in heaven had obviously been persecuted and killed on earth for their faith.
- They now serve God in heaven and God promises that He will dwell among them.

106

- They will never be hungry or thirsty again.
- They will never be tortured by the sun or fire or heat again.
- Christ, as their Shepherd, will take care of them and comfort them.
- As their Shepherd, Christ will lead them to living fountains of water.
- They will have no more sorrow.
- God will wipe away every tear.
- What a great ending to a chapter of revival and God's grace.

REVELATION:
CHAPTER EIGHT

Here, we are introduced to the seventh seal of judgment and the seven trumpets of judgement.

THE SEVENTH SEAL—SILENCE IN HEAVEN

8:1 When He opened the seventh seal, there was silence in heaven for about half an hour.
- Some scholars have written that the introduction to chapter 8 has all the features of a Yon Kippur service from the days of the Jewish temple.
- One Jewish writer said that on Yon Kippur the priest spent about 30 minutes of silence in God's presence.
- The reason for the 30 minutes silence is not stated.
- The events described in verses 2 through 6 are parenthetical events that take place in heaven between the seventh and final seal of judgment and the blowing of the first trumpet of judgment.

THE SEVEN TRUMPETS OF JUDGMENT

8:2 And I saw the seven angels who stand before God, and to them were given seven trumpets.
- The seven seals have been opened and judgments have been poured out by an angry God.
- Following the silence during the seventh seal, the seven angels prepare to blow the seven trumpets to announce further judgments.

- The seventh trumpet will be blown in the middle of the seven year tribulation.
- Listed below are the seven trumpet judgments:

1st trumpet   - Hail, fire and blood rain down from heaven.
2nd trumpet - A burning meteor fell from heaven.
3rd trumpet - The star wormwood poisoned the waters.
4th trumpet - One third of the planet became dark.
5th trumpet - Demons tormented men for five months.
6th trumpet - 2,000,000 demons killed one-third of the population.
7th trumpet - Satan was cast out of the heavens to earth to vent his wrath against the nation of Israel.

PRAYER IN HEAVEN

8:3 Then another angel, having a golden censer, came and stood at the altar. He was given much incense, that he should offer it with the prayers of all the saints upon the golden altar which was before the throne.
- I believe that this angel is the Lord Jesus Christ, our High Priest.
- In the Old Testament the censer was always associated with the High Priest.

8:4 And the smoke of the incense, with the prayers of the saints, ascended before God from the angel's hand.
5 Then the angel took the censer, filled it with fire from the altar, and threw it to the earth. And there were noises, thunderings, lightnings, and an earthquake.
6 So the seven angels who had the seven trumpets prepared themselves to sound.
- After 30 minutes of silence and much prayer, heaven is filled with noises, thunderings, lightnings and an earthquake as the seven angels prepare to blow their trumpets of judgment.

The First Trumpet—Vegetation Destroyed

***8:7** The first angel sounded: And hail and fire followed, mingled with blood, and they were thrown to the earth. And a third of the trees were burned up, and all green grass was burned up.*

- With each of the seven trumpets the judgments get more severe.
- With the first trumpet, hail and fire mingled with blood fell from the sky.
- One third of the trees were burned up and all grass was destroyed.
- This also happened to Sodom and was also one of the ten plagues in Egypt.
- Some writers believe that this will be the result of a nuclear war.

The Second Trumpet—One Third Of The Sea Destroyed

***8:8** Then the second angel sounded: And something like a great mountain burning with fire was thrown into the sea, and a third of the sea became blood.*

***9** And a third of the living creatures in the sea died, and a third of the ships were destroyed.*

- John writes that something like a great mountain burning with fire was cast into the sea.
- This could be a meteor or some kind of nuclear weapon.
- One third of the seas turned to blood.
- One third of the fish died.
- One third of the ships were destroyed.

The Third Trumpet—Poisoned Water

***8:10** Then the third angel sounded: And a great star fell*

from heaven, burning like a torch, and it fell on a third of the rivers and on the springs of water.
11 The name of the star is Wormwood. A third of the waters became wormwood, and many men died from the water, because it was made bitter.

- We don't know whether John saw a literal star or a nuclear warhead.
- He described it as a great star fell from heaven, burning like a torch.
- John had never witnessed atomic and hydrogen bombs, warplanes, military helicopters and nuclear warheads. How would he describe the destruction of the last days?
- One third of the rivers and the springs of water became bitter and many men died from drinking the poisoned water.
- This was in contrast to the time in the wilderness when Moses threw a tree into the bitter waters; they became sweet and God made a covenant of healing with Israel (Exodus 15:25-27).
- This was similar to one of the ten plagues of Egypt.
- In 1823 in the Aleutian Islands there was a volcanic explosion that made the waters so bitter that no one could drink them.

CHERNOBYL MEANS WORMWOOD

- Pauline and I have ministered in the Ukraine several times.
- In their language, the word Chernobyl means Wormwood.
- It was at Chernobyl in Russia that the nuclear plant leaked poisonous nuclear gases and had to be closed.
- Many people died and many more were exposed to the poisonous air.

THE FOURTH TRUMPET
—THE HEAVENS AFFECTED

8:12 And the fourth angel sounded, and the third part of the

sun was struck, a third of the moon, and a third of the
stars, so that a third of them were darkened. A third of the
day did not shine, and likewise the night.
13 And I looked, and I heard an angel flying through the
midst of heaven, saying with a loud voice, "Woe, woe, woe
to the inhabitants of the earth, because of the remaining
blasts of the trumpet of the three angels who are about to
sound.

- In the creation week on the fourth day, the Bible states that God put the lights in the heavens and it was good.
- Now in the fourth trumpet judgment in the seven year tribulation, God darkens one-third of the sun, the moon and the stars.
- This also happened during the plagues of Egypt.
- Similar prophecies were predicted for the last days (Joel 2:30-31).
- In the judgments of the first four trumpets, the seas and the water supply were contaminated, the vegetation was destroyed, and the sun, moon, and stars reduced their light.
- That would cause the entire ecological system to collapse.
- These events are similar to what happened during the sixth seal of judgment.
- These judgments are similar to what will happen during the fifth bowl of judgment in the last half of the seven year tribulation.
- This judgment is similar to the ninth plague in Egypt when darkness lasted three days.

THE ANGEL ANNOUNCES
THREE MORE TRUMPETS

- After the first four trumpets have sounded, an angel flies through the midst of heaven to announce that the last three trumpet judgments will be more severe.
- In the first four judgments, God deals with the material and physical creation.
- In the next three judgments He will deal with His moral creation.

Revelation:
Chapter Nine

In this chapter we meet the demons which arise from the bottomless pit—plus 200,000,000 spirit horses and their riders.

The Fifth Trumpet—The Bottomless Pit Is Opened

9:1 *Then the fifth angel sounded: And I saw a star fallen from heaven to the earth. To him was given the key to the bottomless pit.*

- This star was obviously an angel.
- Pronouns such as "he" and "him" are given to him and he performs certain functions.
- Some scholars teach that this is the devil who is a fallen angel.
- Others teach that it is one of Satan's fallen angels.
- I believe this is one of God's angels, because he was given the key to the abyss.
- None of Satan's fallen angels would be given such authority.

The Bottomless Pit

- God and His angels live in the third heaven (2 Corinthians 12; 2-4).
- Satan and the fallen angels operate in the mid heaven, the second heaven, or what the Bible calls the heavenlies.
- We live on planet earth but there is an area called the abyss, or the bottomless pit under the earth.

• The bottomless pit will be where Satan will be bound during the thousand year's reign of Christ.

9:2 And he opened the bottomless pit, and smoke arose out of the pit like the smoke of a great furnace. So the sun and the air were darkened because of the smoke of the pit.
• When the angel opened the bottomless pit smoke arose out of the pit.
• This suggests that the abyss is a furnace of fire.
• The smoke from the abyss was so thick that it darkened the blazing sun.

THE DEMON LOCUSTS FROM THE PIT

9:3 Then out of the smoke locusts came upon the earth. And to them was given power, as the scorpions of the earth have power.
4 They were commanded not to harm the grass of the earth, or any green thing, or any tree, but only those men who do not have the seal of God on their foreheads.
5 And they were not given authority to kill them, but to torment them for five months. Their torment was like the torment of a scorpion when it strikes a man.
6 In those days men will seek death and will not find it; they will desire to die, and death will flee from them.
• Locusts came out of the smoke which came from the abyss.
• They were commanded not to harm the trees and the vegetation.
• They were commanded to harm only those people who did not have God's seal on their foreheads.
• They could not kill people but could torment them for five months.
• Their torment will feel like the sting of a scorpion.
• The torment will be so severe that people will want to die but will be unable to.

A Description of the Locusts

9:7 The shape of the locusts was like horses prepared for battle. On their heads were crowns of something like gold, and their faces were like the faces of men.

8 They had hair like women's hair, and their teeth were like lions' teeth.

9 And they had breastplates like breastplates of iron, and the sound of their wings was like the sound of chariots with many horses running into battle.

10 They had tails like scorpions, and there were stings in their tails. Their power was to hurt men five months.

11 And they had as king over them the angel of the bottomless pit, whose name in Hebrew is Abaddon, but in Greek he has the name Apollyon.

- These locusts were not ordinary locusts.
- They were obviously either demons or fallen angels.
- They had the sting of scorpions
- They looked like horses preparing for battle.
- On their heads they had crowns that looked like gold.
- Their faces looked like men.
- They had hair that looked like women's hair.
- Their teeth were like lions' teeth.
- They had iron breastplates.
- They had wings that sounded like many chariots and horses preparing for battle.
- They had tails like scorpions with stings in their tails.
- They had a king over them named Abaddon in Hebrew and Apollyon in Greek. This means the destroyer.
- When they were cast into the pit in the past, the sin that caused them to be bound there and loosed at this time is not stated.

9:12 One woe is past. Behold, still two more woes are coming after these things.

THE SIXTH TRUMPET—
ANGELS FROM THE EUPHRATES

9:13 Then the sixth angel sounded: And I heard a voice from the four horns of the golden altar which is before God,

14 saying to the sixth angel who had the trumpet, "Release the four angels who are bound at the great river Euphrates."

15 So the four angels, who had been prepared for the hour and day and month and year, were released to kill a third of mankind.

- These are four fallen angels that have been bound under the river Euphrates.
- This river runs through Iraq and Syria.
- We do not know why they were bound and released at this time.
- They are appointed to kill one third of the world's population at this given moment in the seven year tribulation.
- Some believe that this was the location of the Garden of Eden.
- Some scholars believe this was where the Tower of Babel was built and it will be where the city of Babylon will be built as the Antichrist's headquarters.

A DEMON ARMY OF 200,000,000

9:16 Now the number of the army of the horsemen was two hundred million; I heard the number of them.

17 And thus I saw the horses in the vision: those who sat on them had breastplates of fiery red, hyacinth blue, and sulfur yellow; and the heads of the horses were like the heads of lions; and out of their mouths came fire, smoke, and brimstone.

18 By these three plagues a third of mankind was killed—by the fire and the smoke and the brimstone which came out of their mouths.

117

19 For their power is in their mouth and in their tails; for their tails are like serpents, having heads; and with them they do harm.

- We are now introduced to 200,000,000 spirit horses and their riders.
- They had breastplates that were fiery red, blue and yellow.
- The horses' heads looked like lions.
- Out of their mouths came fire, smoke and brimstone.
- They had destructive power in their tails. Their tails were like serpents that harmed people.
- They killed one third of the world's population.
- They were either spirits of demons or fallen angels assigned to kill men or they were demon spirits sent to influence men to carry out these judgments.

No Repentance

9:20 But the rest of mankind, who were not killed by these plagues, did not repent of the works of their hands, that they should not worship demons, and idols of gold, silver, brass, stone, and wood, which can neither see nor hear nor walk.
9:21 And they did not repent of their murders or their sorceries or their sexual immorality or their thefts.

- In spite of God's judgment, men did not repent of demon worship, occult practices, worshiping idols, murder, drug abuse, immorality and thefts.

Hell on Earth

- During the seven years of tribulation, all hell will be loosed on the earth. This will be especially true in the final three and a half years.

- In the first half of the tribulation, the Antichrist will be busy gaining control over his kingdom of ten nations.
- During the last half of this period, as the leader of the ten nation confederation and other nations he will conquer and control, together with nations which are satanically inspired to join him, he will have authority over the most powerfully destructive military alliance the world has ever known.
- The Bible teaches that in addition to his powerful military base, he will also receive power from Satan himself.
- He will seek to destroy the nation of Israel.
- This will climax at the Battle of Armageddon and the Second Coming of Christ.

REVELATION:
CHAPTER TEN

What is the meaning of the "little book' or scroll? And why was John instructed to "eat it"?

THE MIGHTY ANGEL WITH THE LITTLE BOOK

10:1 I saw still another mighty angel coming down from heaven, clothed with a cloud. And a rainbow was on his head, his face was like the sun, and his feet like pillars of fire.

2 He had a little book open in his hand. And he set his right foot on the sea and his left foot on the land,

3 and cried with a loud voice, as when a lion roars. When he cried out, seven thunders uttered their voices.

- These verses introduce additional parenthetical events.
- They happen between the sixth and seventh trumpet judgments.
- Most prophecy scholars agree that this angel is the Lord Jesus Christ Himself.
- The Bible states that He cried with a loud voice as when a lion roars.
- Christ was introduced as the Lion of the Tribe of Judah (chapter 5:5).
- There are also several Old Testament Scriptures which refer to Christ roaring in wrath as a lion in the Day of the Lord.
- This Mighty Angel, the Lord Jesus Christ is clothed with a cloud.

- A rainbow was on His head, His face was like the sun, His feet were like pillars of fire.
- In chapter 5: 5-7, Christ takes the seven sealed scroll out of the Father's right hand.
- In chapter 6:1 to 8:1, Christ breaks the seven seals that bind the scroll.
- He holds the open scroll in His right hand so that the contents inside the scroll can be revealed.
- As the omnipotent King, He places one foot on the earth and one foot on the sea.

THE VOICE OF THE LION OF JUDAH

10:4 Now when the seven thunders uttered their voices, I was about to write; but I heard a voice from heaven saying to me, "Seal up the things which the seven thunders uttered, and do not write them."

5 The angel whom I saw standing on the sea and on the land raised up his hand to heaven

6 and swore by Him who lives forever and ever, who created heaven and the things that are in it, the earth and the things that are in it, and the sea and the things that are in it, that there should be delay no longer,

- When He spoke, seven thunders utter their voices, John is forbidden to write what the thunders uttered.
- God spoke in the voice of thunder on Mount Sinai (Exodus 20:15).
- God also spoke miraculously with a voice of thunder when He spoke to Christ (John 12:28-29).
- His voice roars like the Lion King, which relates Him to the Lion of Judah.
- Christ swore by Himself.

- In at least 50 Scriptures it says that God swore or God swore by Himself.
- Christ, the Creator commands John what to write and what not to write.
- When the Bible says that there should be delay no longer, it means that God is going to fulfill immediately the mystery of God, recorded in verse 7.

10:7 but in the days of the sounding of the seventh angel, when he is about to sound, the mystery of God would be finished, as He declared to His servants the prophets.
- The Bible does not reveal what the Mystery of God is.
- It states simply that God will not delay it any longer.
- Many scholars believe that it refers to God's defeat of the devil when He casts him to the earth (chapter 12).

JOHN EATS THE LITTLE BOOK

10:8 Then the voice which I heard from heaven spoke to me again and said, "Go, take the little book which is open in the hand of the angel who stands on the sea and on the earth."
9 So I went to the angel and said to him, "Give me the little book" And he said to me, "Take and eat it; and it will make your stomach bitter, but it will be as sweet as honey in your mouth."
10 Then I took the little book out of the angel's hand and ate it, and it was as sweet as honey in my mouth. But when I had eaten it, my stomach became bitter.
11 And he said to me, "You must prophesy again about many peoples, nations, tongues, and kings."
- Any revelation from God is sweet as we receive it but when we realize it is a message of judgment it becomes bitter.

• To eat the book is a Hebraism which means to receive knowledge.

• John was told to eat the little book, or scroll and that he must "prophesy again about many peoples."

• This he did in the remaining chapters of the Book of Revelation.

• John has also prophesied every time anyone reads the Book of Revelation or whenever anyone preaches from its pages.

• He is prophesying to you even now as you read this book.

Revelation:
Chapter Eleven

In this chapter the two witnesses are introduced and their purpose revealed.

The Jewish Rebuilt Temple

11:1 Then I was given a reed like a measuring rod. And the angel stood, saying, "Rise and measure the temple of God, the altar, and those who worship there."
• John is commanded to measure the temple.
• In the Scriptures there are five temples:
1. Solomon's temple (1 Kings 5-8).
   • This replaced Moses' tabernacle in the wilderness after the Israelites arrived in the Promised Land.
   • This temple was destroyed by King Nebuchadnezzar of the Empire of Babylon in approximately 590 B.C.
2. Zerubbabel's temple (Hagaii 1-2).
   • This was rebuilt after Israel's 70 year captivity in Babylon.
   • This temple was desecrated by Antiochus Epipanes, a Greco-Syrian ruler.
   • He offered a pig on the altar.
   • This desecration prefigures the Abomination of Desolation which will be built by the False Prophet for the Antichrist in the rebuilt temple in Jerusalem.
3. Herod's temple (John 2:19-20).
   • This was the temple in Jesus' day.
   • It was destroyed by Titus and the Roman armies in A.D. 70.

4. Another Jewish temple will be built in the near future.
   • It will be used by the Jews until it is taken over by the Antichrist in the last three and a half years of the seven year tribulation.
   • This is the temple referred to in chapter 11:1. See also Daniel 8:27 and 2 Thessalonians 2: 3-4.
   • Verse 2, below states that this temple will have no outer court for the Gentiles as there was in the previous temples.
   • The reason John gives is that the Gentiles, or the Antichrist and his subjects, will trample under foot, or persecute and desecrate the city of Jerusalem and the outer court of the temple for the final three and a half years of the tribulation.
5. The Millennial temple (Ezekiel 40-48).
   • This will be built in Jerusalem when Christ reigns from that city for 1,000 years.

11:2 But leave out the court which is outside the temple, and do not measure it, for it has been given to the Gentiles. And they will tread the holy city underfoot for forty-two months.

• When the Jews build their temple in the near future animal sacrifice and the priesthood will be reintroduced.
• The Bible does not state whether the temple will be built before or after the Rapture.
• We do not know how long it will be after the Rapture before the Antichrist will be revealed to make his peace pact with Israel.
• We do not know how long the temple will be used by the Jews before the peace pact is broken by the Antichrist.
• The Jews have been making plans to build this temple for several years.

THE TWO WITNESSES INTRODUCED

11:3 And I will give power to my two witnesses, and they will prophesy one thousand two hundred and sixty days (three and a half years), clothed in sackcloth."
4 These are the two olive trees and the two lampstands standing before the God of the earth.

- Earlier in this book I said that God has always had a witness on the earth.
- After the Rapture, the 144,000 Jewish evangelists were God's witnesses.
- They were on earth in chapter 7 but they are in heaven in chapter 14.
- I believe that they are raptured in the middle of the tribulation.
- The two witnesses will become God's witnesses on the earth for the final half of the seven year tribulation.

THEIR MIRACULOUS POWER, DEATH, RESURRECTION, AND ASCENSION

11:5 And if anyone wants to harm them, fire proceeds from their mouth and devours their enemies. And if anyone wants to harm them, he must be killed in this manner.
6 These have power to shut heaven, so that no rain falls in the days of their prophecy; and they have power over waters to turn them to blood, and to strike the earth with all plagues, as often as they desire.
7 When they finish their testimony, the beast that ascends out of the bottomless pit will make war against them, overcome them, and kill them.
8 And their dead bodies will lie in the street of the great city which spiritually is called Sodom and Egypt, where also our Lord was crucified.

9 Then those from the peoples, tribes, tongues, and nations will see their dead bodies three-and-a-half days, and not allow their dead bodies to be put into graves.

10 And those who dwell on the earth will rejoice over them, make merry, and send gifts to one another, because these two prophets tormented those who dwell on the earth

11 Now after the three-and-a-half days the breath of life from God entered them, and they stood on their feet, and great fear fell on those who saw them

12 And they heard a loud voice from heaven saying to them, "Come up here." And they ascended to heaven in a cloud, and their enemies saw them.

13 In the same hour there was a great earthquake, and a tenth of the city fell. In the earthquake seven thousand people were killed, and the rest were afraid and gave glory to the God of heaven.

- The two witnesses are two mortal men with supernatural power.
- They will witness for Christ during the final three and a half years of the seven year tribulation.
- They are symbolized by the two olive trees and the two lampstands standing before the God of the earth (Zechariah 4: 1-14; Revelation 11:4).
- This means they were in heaven when Zechariah prophesied about them 500 years before Christ.
- They wore sackcloth as a sign of mourning because of coming judgment.
- If any man tries to kill them, fire comes out of their mouths and destroys their enemies.
- In whatever way their enemies seek to hurt them, their enemies will be killed in the same manner.
- They will have power to stop the rain, turn waters to blood and smite the earth with all plagues.
- These plagues will be in addition to the judgments poured out by an angry God.

- At the end of the seven year tribulation the Antichrist will kill them.
- The people will refuse them a decent burial.
- Their dead bodies will lie in the streets of Jerusalem and the people will celebrate their death.
- After three and a half days the Spirit of life, the Holy Spirit, resurrects them; they stand on their feet and they are raptured to heaven.
- John heard a loud voice saying, come up here and the two witnesses were caught up in a cloud in the sight of their enemies.
- This will cause great fear as men witness it.
- At that moment another earthquake will strike the city of Jerusalem; one-tenth of the city will be destroyed and 7,000 people will die.
- Jerusalem is called Sodom and Egypt because the sexual immorality of Sodom and the idolatry of Egypt will be prevalent on the earth after the Rapture.
- When they have finished their witnessing ministry, they are killed by the Antichrist who is satanically empowered by a beast, the spirit of a fallen angel who comes out of the pit (verse 7).
- When the Bible refers to the beast out of the pit, it does not mean that the Antichrist himself will come out of the abyss. The Bible does not teach reincarnation.

WHO ARE THE TWO WITNESSES?

- According to Malachi 4:4-5, one of the two witnesses is definitely Elijah.
- Some say they are Elijah and Moses because they both appeared on the Mount of Transfiguration and Moses performed the same miracles described above in Egypt.
- I believe the second witness is Enoch because he and Elijah are the only two men who have ever gone to heaven without dying.

- The Bible states that, *It is appointed unto man once to die* (Hebrews 9:27).
- Both Elijah and Enoch will die their appointed death at the hands of the Antichrist.
- Enoch was taught to be the second witness in the writings of some of the early church fathers and in the writings in the apocrypha.
- These writings were not included in the canon of Scripture but they are interesting and helpful to document the teachings of the early church.

EVENTS DURING THE BLOWING OF THE SEVENTH TRUMPET

11:14 The second woe is past. Behold, the third woe is coming quickly.
- The third woe will be the seventh and final trumpet of judgment.

THE KINGDOM PROCLAIMED

11:15 Then the seventh angel sounded: and there were loud voices in heaven, saying, "The kingdoms of this world have become the kingdoms of our Lord and of His Christ, and He shall reign forever and ever!"
- The fact that Satan is about to be cast out of the heavens means that Christ's Kingdom will soon be established on the earth.
- Verse 15 is a prophetic insert because Christ will not rule over the nations until He returns to earth.

11:16 And the twenty-four elders who sat before God on their thrones fell on their faces and worshiped God,
17 saying: "We give You thanks, O Lord God Almighty, The One who is and who was and who is to come, Because You

129

have taken Your great power and reigned.
- The 24 elders are worshiping the Lord because the Bible says He has reigned.
- This is another prophetic insert because Christ will not reign until the seven year tribulation is over and Jesus returns to earth to fight at the Battle of Armageddon and establish His Kingdom on earth.

THE NATIONS ARE ANGRY

11:18 The nations were angry, and Your wrath has come, And the time of the dead, that they should be judged, And that You should reward Your servants the prophets and the saints, And those who fear Your name, small and great, And should destroy those who destroy the earth. "
- The nations which were angry are the nations of the Antichrist who will be defeated at the Battle of Armageddon when they declare war against the Lord Jesus Christ.
- They will be angry because the Antichrist promised them that if they followed him they would win the victory and now they realize that the Antichrist lied to them.
- After their defeat Christ will judge the nations.
- The sheep nations will be those nations who have allied with Israel against the Antichrist.
- The sheep nations will enter the Kingdom. Christ and His Bride will rule over them in the Millennium.
- The goat nations will be those nations who allied with the Antichrist against Israel and her allies.
- The goat nations will be destroyed (Matthew 25:31-46).

THE JUDGMENT SEAT OF CHRIST

- Verse 18 teaches that Christ will judge and reward the

following at the Judgment Seat of Christ:
The resurrected dead.
God's servants, the prophets.
The saints.
Those who fear God's name, small and great.

THE TEMPLE OPENED IN HEAVEN

11:19 Then the temple of God was opened in heaven, and the ark of His covenant was seen in His temple. And there were lightnings, noises, thunderings, an earthquake, and great hail.

- As we have stated several times there is a temple in heaven with an Ark of the Covenant.
- This was the Ark of the Covenant from which Moses patterned the ark in the tabernacle in the wilderness.
- The temple in heaven had the furnishings of the tabernacle of Moses and the temple of Solomon.
- The one piece of furniture that was missing in the heavenly temple was the veil because we now have access to God because of the blood of the Lamb.
- Lightnings, noises, thunderings, an earthquake, and great hail signified additional judgment about to fall to the earth.
- The Jewish historian Josephus wrote that the door of the temple in Jerusalem opened miraculously four years before the temple was destroyed in A.D. 70. He stated that this was a sign of God's coming judgment.

REVELATION:
CHAPTER TWELVE

T his chapter deals with spiritual warfare, including Satan and his angels being cast to the earth.

WHO IS THE SUN CLOTHED WOMAN?

12:1 Now a great sign appeared in heaven: a woman clothed with the sun, with the moon under her feet, and on her head a garland of twelve stars.
- The following four women are mentioned in the Book of Revelation.
    1. Jezebel, the false prophetess in chapter 2 verse 20.
    2. The Bride, the Lamb's wife.
    3. The sun clothed woman described above.
    4. The harlot of Revelation 13, which is a false and deceptive religious system.
- To avoid any misunderstanding about the identity of the sun clothed woman, we must note that this event occurs during the seventh trumpet judgment in the middle of the future seven year tribulation.
- Thus, she cannot be a woman of past history.
- John saw the sign while he was in heaven but the woman appeared on earth.
- There has been some speculation as to the identity of the woman.
- The Christian Scientists claim she was their founder, Mary Baker Eddy.
- Some teach that the woman is the church.

- Others teach it is only the members of the church who have been baptized in the Spirit, or other special elect groups in the church.
- However, the church is the church, the Body of Christ. There are no special elect or favored groups within the church. There is only one body.
- Some believe she is the Virgin Mary.
- Others have been nominated from past history but the woman will be revealed in the middle of the future seven year tribulation.

THE WOMAN IS THE NATION OF ISRAEL

- Israel is often referred to as a woman, married to God in the Old Testament.
- The woman was clothed with the sun, with the moon under her feet, and on her head a garland of 12 stars.
- Joseph's dream explains that the sun, moon, and 12 stars symbolized Israel in Genesis 37: 9-11.
- Michael was assigned to fight against the dragon and Michael is the archangel assigned to fight for Israel.

LABOR PAINS AND THE BIRTH OF THE MAN CHILD

12:2 Then being with child, she cried out in labor and in pain to give birth.

- In Matthew 24, Jesus predicted that the first part of the tribulation would be the beginning of sorrows.
- The word sorrows is the Greek word for travail or labor pains.
- There are several prophecies in the Old Testament which speak of Israel in travail (Isaiah 66:7-8; Jeremiah 30:6-9; Micah 5:3).

THE FIERY RED DRAGON, WITH SEVEN HEADS AND TEN HORNS

12:3 And another sign appeared in heaven: behold, a great, fiery red dragon having seven heads and ten horns, and seven diadems on his heads.

- The word, dragon is used 13 times in the Book of Revelation.
- The dragon refers to the devil.
- The seven heads with the seven crowns refer to the seven world empires which have been under Satan's control.
- They are Egypt, Assyria, Babylon, Medes and Persians, Greece, and Rome.
- The ten horns are ten nations that are yet to be formed within the boundary of the former Roman Empire.
- All of these world powers have persecuted Israel in the past and the seventh empire, the ten nation confederation, will do so when they are formed in the near future.
- When the Antichrist has gained total power over ten nations in the middle of the seven year tribulation, they will become the eighth world power which will be destroyed at the Battle of Armageddon when Jesus returns to earth to establish His Kingdom with His world headquarters in Jerusalem.

SATAN AND HIS ANGELS CAST TO THE EARTH

12:4 His tail drew a third of the stars of heaven and threw them to the earth. And the dragon stood before the woman who was ready to give birth, to devour her Child as soon as it was born.

- The third of the stars which the dragon drew to the earth refer to the third of the angels that joined Lucifer in his initial rebellion against God (Isaiah 14:12-15).
- Now the dragon and the fallen angels, who have been cast down to the earth seek to destroy national Israel and her child (the manchild) as soon as it was born.

WHO IS THE MANCHILD?

12:5 She bore a male Child who was to rule all nations with a rod of iron. And her Child was caught up to God and His throne.

- The manchild is a symbol of the 144,000 Jewish evangelists because the woman was national Israel; therefore her baby boy would be part of national Israel.
- The baby cannot be the birth of Christ as some teach because the manchild will not be born until the middle of the future seven year tribulation.
- The manchild cannot be the church because the church was raptured before the seven years of tribulation.
- The woman in this chapter appears in the middle of the future seven year tribulation (verse 6).
- Both the manchild and the 144,000 are raptured.
- They are on earth in chapter 7 and are in heaven in chapter 14.
- There is no other group apart from the 144,000 which would fit the description of the manchild.

ISRAEL'S PROTECTION IN THE ROCK CITY OF PETRA

12:6 Then the woman fled into the wilderness, where she has a place prepared by God, that they should feed her there one thousand two hundred and sixty days.

- As the dragon inspires the Antichrist to break his peace pact and attempt to destroy the nation of Israel, many of the Jews escape to the land of Jordan in the rock city of Sela or Petra as it was called by the Romans.
- Petra means a rock, a boulder or a stronghold (Isaiah 16:1-5; 26:20-21; 63:1-5).
- It is also called Bozrah (Amos 1:12; Isaiah 34:5-6; 63:1-5; Jeremiah 48:24; 49:13, 22).
- Petra is in Mount Seir, near Mount Hor in the land of Edom and Moab in the wilderness where Israel wandered for 40 years as they left the land of Egypt.

- For hundreds of years Petra was lost to the civilized world until it was rediscovered in the year 1812 by a man called Burckhardt.
- In Daniel 11:36-45, the Bible prophesies that Edom and Moab in Jordan and Amon, the capital of Jordan will escape the hand of the Antichrist in the future tribulation.
- This will be to allow them to protect those Jews who flee from their home land to escape the hand of the Antichrist's reign of terror.

ACCESS TO PETRA

- My wife and I have visited Petra many times.
- It can be reached only by a narrow passage way.
- The only access is to walk or ride on the back of an animal.
- The rocks are so high, they blot out the sun and if you look down, you see a sheer precipice.
- Once you arrive inside the Rock City you discover a vast space which is capable of protecting many, many people.

WAR IN HEAVEN AND SATAN CAST OUT

12:7 And war broke out in heaven: Michael and his angels fought with the dragon; and the dragon and his angels fought,

8 but they did not prevail, nor was a place found for them in heaven any longer.

9 So the great dragon was cast out, that serpent of old, called the Devil and Satan, who deceives the whole world; he was cast to the earth, and his angels were cast out with him.

- When Lucifer rebelled against God, he was cast out of the third heaven into the second heaven (Isaiah 14:12-15), or what the Bible calls the heavenlies.

- One third of the angels joined him in that rebellion and they are the fallen angels.
- Verses 7 through 9 teach that Satan and his fallen angels will be cast out of the heavenlies to the earth in the middle of the future seven year tribulation.

THE ACCUSER CAST DOWN

12:10 Then I heard a loud voice saying in heaven, "Now salvation, and strength, and the kingdom of our God, and the power of His Christ have come, for the accuser of our brethren, who accused them before our God day and night, has been cast down.

11 And they overcame him by the blood of the Lamb and by the word of their testimony, and they did not love their lives to the death.

12 Therefore rejoice, O heavens, and you who dwell in them! Woe to the inhabitants of the earth and the sea! For the devil has come down to you, having great wrath, because he knows that he has a short time."

- The devil means the accuser or the slanderer.
- Satan means the adversary.
- In verse 10 he is called the accuser of the brethren.

SPIRITUAL WARFARE

- While the Book of Revelation is a prophecy of coming events, the following are exciting truths which you can apply today in dealing with the enemy:
- Although Satan was cast out of God's heaven in past eternity, Job teaches us that he still has access to God's throne.
- His purpose is to accuse the believers day and night.
- However, if we fail or sin in any way, we can immediately claim the protection of 1 John 1:9, *If we confess our sins,*

God is faithful and just to forgive our sins and cleanse us of all unrighteousness.
- Once Satan is cast down to the earth he will not be able to accuse us any more, because he will not have access to God's throne.
- In the meantime, when the devil reminds you of your past, you remind him of his future.
- Stand fast in the truth of Romans 8:1, *There is therefore now no condemnation.*

THE MILITANT CHURCH

- Although Michael and his angels have the power to cast the devil out of the heavenlies, God, in His will and wisdom wanted the tribulation saints on earth to join Michael and God's angels and be involved in spiritual warfare.
- The Bible says, They (the tribulation saints) overcame him (the devil) by the blood of the Lamb and the word of their testimony (chapter 12:11).
- The blood of Jesus is a powerful weapon to use against the enemy.
- Other weapons are the Name of Jesus, the sword of the Spirit, the spoken Word of God and praise.

SATAN'S TIME IS LIMITED

- When Satan is cast to the earth, the Bible states that he will have great wrath because he knows that he has a short time.
- He will have only three and a half years before he is bound in the pit for 1,000 years.
- After being bound in the pit he will be cast into the Lake of Fire for all eternity.
- During his limited time on earth, he will give his power to the Antichrist to persecute the Jewish nation and try to destroy them.

MORE PERSECUTION AND MORE PROTECTION

12:13 Now when the dragon saw that he had been cast to the earth, he persecuted the woman who gave birth to the male Child.

- When Satan could not attack the 144,000 because they were raptured to heaven, he resumed his hostility against the woman, the nation of Israel.
- For the final three and a half years of the seven year tribulation, Israel will suffer the greatest persecution in history.

THE WINGS OF AN EAGLE

12:14 But the woman was given two wings of a great eagle, that she might fly into the wilderness to her place, where she is nourished for a time and times and half a time, from the presence of the serpent.

- Some prophecy preachers teach that the great eagle refers to the United States of America.
- I hope that America will always be a friend of Israel, but it is stretching the truth to teach that the wings of an eagle refer to America.
- God has used the symbol of an eagle's wings to lead, protect and deliver Israel several times in the Old Testament.
- The term "time and times and half a time" in verse 14, is also found in the book of Daniel and refers to the final three and a half years of the tribulation.

NAMES OF THE ENEMY

- The Book of Revelation refers to the enemy as the devil, Satan, the dragon and the serpent.

WATER SYMBOLIZES THE ANTICHRIST'S ARMIES

12:15 So the serpent spewed water out of his mouth like a flood after the woman, that he might cause her to be carried away by the flood.

16 But the earth helped the woman, and the earth opened its mouth and swallowed up the flood which the dragon had spewed out of his mouth.

- God will cause the earth to open up supernaturally and swallow the Antichrist's armies just as He did to Korah and his company in Numbers 16: 29-35.
- The water and the flood refer to the armies of the Antichrist.
- They will be satanically inspired to make one final attempt to annihilate the nation of Israel at the Battle of Armageddon.

A JEWISH REMNANT PRESERVED

12:17 And the dragon was enraged with the woman, and he went to make war with the rest of her offspring, who keep the commandments of God and have the testimony of Jesus Christ.

- The offspring Jews are the Jews who remained in Israel rather than fleeing to the Rock City of Petra in Jordan.
- These remnant Jews turned to Christ and probably were influenced by the ministry and the rapture of the 144,000 Jewish evangelists and the testimony of the two witnesses.

REVELATION:
CHAPTER THIRTEEN

In this revealing chapter we learn much more concerning the Antichrist, the mark of the beast, and who the final victor will be.

THE BEAST OUT OF THE SEA—WHO IS HE?

13:1 Then I stood on the sand of the sea. And I saw a beast rising up out of the sea, having seven heads and ten horns, and on his horns ten crowns, and on his heads a blasphemous name.
2 Now the beast which I saw was like a leopard, his feet were like the feet of a bear, and his mouth like the mouth of a lion. The dragon gave him his power, his throne, and great authority.

- In his vision, John saw himself standing on the beaches of the Mediterranean Sea, around which some of the ten nations over which the Antichrist will reign are located.
- John saw a beast rising up out of the sea of humanity. This is the Antichrist.
- There are 17 titles in the Bible to describe the personality and the activity of the Antichrist. One of those titles is the beast.
- The Antichrist will be vile, wild, vicious, and ferocious in his satanic hatred for Israel and all people who refuse to take the mark of the beast and 666, the number of his name.
- The Antichrist is a mortal man.

He Comes from Revised Rome
and Revised Greece

- He wears seven heads and ten horns with ten crowns on the horns.
- This suggests that his kingdom will be in the geographical area of the seven past world empires, namely, Egypt, Assyria, Babylon, Medes and Persia, Greece, Rome, and revised Rome which will be where the ten nation confederation will be formed.
- The seven heads were not crowned but the ten horns were.
- Obviously Satan has controlled all of the past world empires that were hostile to Israel, but the ten nation confederacy over which the Antichrist will reign before the Battle of Armageddon and the Second Coming of Christ will become a world power (symbolized by the crowns) only after they are actually formed. The Antichrist comes from one of them.
- He overcomes three of these nations and assumes complete power over all ten by the middle of the seven year tribulation.
- The Book of Revelation deals primarily with the ten horns, or the ten nations of the Antichrist's kingdom and their hostility to Israel.
- The ten horns are crowned because they will be the political and military power base of the Antichrist.
- Most prophecy scholars refer to the ten nations as the revived, or the revised Roman Empire.
- Once the ten nations are formed and the Antichrist rules supreme over them, they become the eighth world power referred to in chapter 17.
- Verse 1 above states that he will look like a leopard, which according to Daniel 7:6 symbolizes Greece.

- Daniel 8 teaches that the ten nations will be reduced to four which made up ancient Greece.
- The four divisions of the old Grecian Empire would be known today as Greece, Turkey, Syria, and Egypt.
- Daniel 11 reduces the nations from four to two, Egypt and Syria, and teaches that the Antichrist will come from the northern nation of those two, namely, Syria.

THE POWER AND THE DESTRUCTION OF THE ANTICHRIST

- The Antichrist will receive his power, his authority and his throne from Satan.
- During Christ's temptation in the wilderness, Satan offered Him the kingdoms of the world if He would worship him. Jesus said, No.
- The devil will offer them to the Antichrist under the same conditions. The Antichrist will say, Yes.
- The Antichrist, the False Prophet, and those nations they lead, will be destroyed at the Battle of Armageddon at the Second Coming of Christ.

ANTICHRIST WILL NOT BE ASSASSINATED AND RESURRECTED

13:3 And I saw one of his heads as if it had been mortally wounded, and his deadly wound was healed. And all the world marveled and followed the beast.
- Some prophecy preachers teach that the Antichrist will be killed and resurrected from the dead to imitate the death and resurrection of Christ.
- The Bible does not state that the Antichrist was killed and resurrected, it states that one of his heads was mortally wounded and healed.

143

- That means that one of the world empires died, or was overthrown in past world history and revived.
- We will examine this truth when we study chapter 17.

THE ANTICHRIST WILL NOT RULE THE WORLD

- Another fallacy that is commonly taught is that the Antichrist will rule the entire world. He will not.
- In spite of verse 3, which states that all the world marveled and followed the beast, consider the following facts.

THE MARK OF THE BEAST

- According to verse 15, the False Prophet will assassinate all peoples who refuse to worship the Antichrist.
- According to chapter 14 verse 9, the Bible teaches that those who do worship the Antichrist or take the mark of the beast, God will destroy.
- The logical question is: If the Antichrist kills those who refuse to worship him and if God destroys those who do, who will be left to populate the earth during the Millennium?

THE ANTICHRIST WILL NOT RULE THE SHEEP NATIONS

- In Matthew 25, Jesus taught that the sheep nations would ally with Israel and oppose the Antichrist.
- The goat nations would oppose Israel and ally with the Antichrist.
- This proves that the Antichrist will not rule the sheep nations and therefore, he does not rule worldwide.
- Daniel 11:41 states that the land of Jordan will escape the control of the Antichrist.

- Jordan is a neighboring nation to Israel.
- Jordan will be a friend to Israel in the seven year tribulation.
- If the Antichrist does not rule the nation of Jordan, he obviously does not rule the world.

THE ANTICHRIST WILL DEFEAT RUSSIA

- Many Bible scholars believe that the Antichrist will invade Israel and be attacked by Russia.
- The Antichrist will defeat Russia's attack and as the Gog of Russia (Ezekiel 38 and 39) with other nations allying with him, he will attack Israel the second time.
- Russia was not part of the former Roman Empire, nor the former Grecian Empire.
- The Antichrist must defeat Russia to become the Gog or leader of Russia.
- The defeat of Russia by the Antichrist will lead to the Battle of Armageddon.
- If he does not initially rule over Russia, he does not have a worldwide kingdom.

WORDS INSPIRED BY DEMONS

- In Revelation 16:13-16, the Bible speaks of demon spirits, like frogs, coming out of the mouths of the dragon, the Antichrist, and the False Prophet.
- They will use satanically inspired words to influence other nations to ally with the Antichrist and oppose Christ at the Battle of Armageddon.
- If the Antichrist ruled the world, these nations would obey his command automatically.

OTHER EXAMPLES FROM THE BIBLE

- When Jesus was born, the Bible says the whole world was taxed. This was not the whole world, but the whole Roman world.
- When Paul wrote to the Roman church, in chapter 1 verse 8 he said, *Your faith is spoken of throughout the whole world.* It was not the whole world, but the whole Christian world.
- In verse 4, the question is asked, *Who is able to make war with him* (with the Antichrist)? If the Antichrist was a worldwide dictator, such a question would be unnecessary.
- Thus, when the Bible states that "Power was given him over all kingdoms and tongues and nations" (verse 7), it refers to all the kingdoms, tongues and nations under the Antichrist's control.
- The prophet Zechariah teaches that even some of the goat nations, such as Egypt, will not take the mark of the beast and be killed. He prophesies that everyone that is left of all the nations which came against Jerusalem (in preparation for the Battle of Armageddon) shall even go up from year to year to worship the King, the Lord of hosts and to keep the Feast of Tabernacles (Zechariah 14:16-21).
- In Daniel 11:40-45 it says that the land of Egypt shall not escape him (the Antichrist).
- Thus, if Egypt is controlled by the Antichrist and some Egyptians enter the Millennium, they obviously did not take the mark of the beast (chapter 14:9-12).

HELL'S TRINITY

13:4 So they worshiped the dragon who gave authority to the beast; and they worshiped the beast, saying, "Who is like the beast? Who is able to make war with him?"

- Heaven's Trinity is God the Father, God the Son, and God the Holy Spirit.
- Chapter 13 introduces Hell's trinity, the dragon, the beast out of the sea (the Antichrist), and the beast out of the earth (the False Prophet).

THE ANTICHRIST BLASPHEMES GOD

13:5 And he was given a mouth speaking great things and blasphemies, and he was given authority to continue for forty-two months.
6 Then he opened his mouth in blasphemy against God, to blaspheme His name, His tabernacle, and those who dwell in heaven.

- According to 2 Thessalonians 2, the Antichrist will establish his throne in the rebuilt temple in Jerusalem.
- He will be worshiped as God.
- In Revelation 13:5-6, the Bible predicts that He will blaspheme God, His Name, His tabernacle, or His dwelling place, and those who dwell in heaven and he will continue for 42 months, or three and a half years.

WAR WITH THE SAINTS

13:7 It was granted to him to make war with the saints and overcome them. And authority was given him over every tribe, tongue, and nation.

- The Bible states that the Antichrist makes war with the saints and overcame them.
- The Old Testament Israelites are called saints, so verse 7 could mean that the Antichrist declared war on the Jews and defeated some of them.
- Or, it could mean that the Antichrist will assassinate more of the tribulation saints.
- It undoubtedly refers to both.

147

The Lamb's Book of Life

13:8 All who dwell on the earth will worship him, whose names have not been written in the Book of Life of the Lamb slain from the foundation of the world.

- Those people who refuse to worship the Antichrist will be martyred during the seven year tribulation.
- Their names, and the names of the saints of all ages will be written in the Lamb's Book of Life.

13:9 If anyone has an ear, let him hear.
10 He who leads into captivity shall go into captivity; he who kills with the sword must be killed with the sword. Here is the patience and the faith of the saints.

Christ the Victor

- Some versions translate verse 10, *He who is destined to go into captivity (to go into prison) will go into captivity (will go into prison); he that is destined to die by the sword will be killed by the sword.*
- Thus, while the Antichrist and his armies will win many battles, they will ultimately be defeated by King Jesus at the Battle of Armageddon.
- Verse 10 calls for the tribulation saints to persevere in faith.

The Second Beast out of the Earth—Who Is He?

13:11 Then I saw another beast coming up out of the earth, and he had two horns like a lamb and spoke like a dragon.
12 And he exercises all the authority of the first beast in his presence, and causes the earth and those who dwell in it to worship the first beast, whose deadly wound was healed.

13 He performs great signs, so that he even makes fire come down from heaven on the earth in the sight of men.

14 And he deceives those who dwell on the earth by those signs which he was granted to do in the sight of the beast, telling those who dwell on the earth to make an image to the beast who was wounded by the sword and lived.

15 He was granted power to give breath to the image of the beast, that the image of the beast should both speak and cause as many as would not worship the image of the beast to be killed.

16 He causes all, both small and great, rich and poor, free and slave, to receive a mark on their right hand or on their foreheads,

17 and that no one may buy or sell except one who has the mark or the name of the beast, or the number of his name.

18 Here is wisdom. Let him who has understanding calculate the number of the beast, for it is the number of a man: His number is 666.

THE FALSE PROPHET

- The first beast, the Antichrist, is a political and a military leader.
- The second beast, the False Prophet, is a religious leader.
- The first beast, the Antichrist, comes out of the sea; this beast, the False Prophet, comes out of the earth.
- In Daniel 7:3 and 7:17, the Bible refers to the beast (the Antichrist) coming out of the earth and out of the sea, so coming out of the earth or coming out of the sea mean the same thing.

FACTS ABOUT THE FALSE PROPHET

- He is a man, like the Antichrist.

149

- He will be a religious leader.
- He had two horns like a lamb (a religious leader) but spoke like a dragon (Satan).
- He will have the same power and authority as the first beast (the Antichrist).
- He will influence people to worship the Antichrist.
- He will perform great miracles and even cause fire to fall from heaven.
- Thus, he will deceive the people by duplicating the miracle of the two witnesses.

THE ABOMINATION OF DESOLATION

- The False Prophet will influence people to build an image of the Antichrist in the rebuilt Jewish temple and will lead them to worship the image.
- This is the Abomination of Desolation (Matthew 24:15 and Daniel 9:27).
- He will have supernatural power to give life to the image so that the image can speak.
- He will cause people to die if they refuse to worship the image of the Antichrist.

SIX, SIX, SIX—THE NUMBER OF HIS NAME

- He will control business and commerce in the kingdom of the Antichrist by refusing people to buy and sell if they do not have the mark of the beast in their right hand or their forehead or 666 the number of the name of the Antichrist.
- There are computer systems which can store information on 10 trillion human beings.
- We are heading toward a cashless society and it is probable that even credit cards will be not be used under the reign of the Antichrist.

THE FALSE PROPHET—AN APOSTATE POPE?

- Some scholars and even some Roman Catholic theologians believe that the False Prophet will be an Apostate Pope.
- They believe that through his miraculous powers and visions of the Virgin Mary, he will unite the millions of Muslims in the five Middle Eastern nations in the eastern division of the ten nation confederation and the millions of Roman Catholics in the five European nations in the western division of the ten nation confederation into one religion.

THE KORAN, JESUS, AND THE VIRGIN MARY?

- Many Christians are not aware that the Koran, the Muslim's holy book respects both Jesus and His mother Mary.
- While there are many teachings on which the Christians and Muslims do not agree, we all agree that Abraham is our common father of faith.
- It may interest Christians to know that Jesus is mentioned in the Koran 97 times, far more than Muhammad is mentioned.
- Listed below are some additional, interesting facts that are mentioned in the Koran:
- Jesus was born of a virgin.
- Jesus is called the Son of Mary.
- The angel Gabriel announced Jesus' supernatural birth.
- Mary was chosen and purified above all women of all nations.
- Jesus had no earthly father.
- Jesus is called the word of God.
- Jesus is called the Messiah.
- Jesus was empowered by the Holy Spirit.
- Jesus healed the sick.
- Jesus raised the dead back to life.
- Jesus will be held in honor in this world and the world hereafter.

- Jesus is without sin and is protected from the evil one.
- Jesus will come back on the Day of Judgment.
- Jesus is Mary's holy child.

A FALSE RELIGION

- Roman Catholics and Muslims both believe in Jesus and in Mary.
- Both religions are fascinated by Mary's alleged vision of Fatima.
- Muhammad named one of his daughters Fatima.
- The Catholic theologians who believe that the False Prophet will be an apostate Pope believe that the miracles performed by the False Prophet, together with visions of the Virgin Mary will be the common denominators to unite these two great world religions.

THE ISLAMIC MAHDI AND THE ANTICHRIST

- According to Islamic beliefs, there are some striking similarities between the final prophet of Islam and the Antichrist.
- He is called "the Expected one."
- He will appear just before the end of the world.
- He will come during the time of tribulation.
- He will come from the east.
- He will come riding on a white horse.
- He will be a great military leader.
- Those who do not obey him will be beaten and beheaded.
- He will rule for seven years.

REVELATION:
CHAPTER FOURTEEN

Ｗhat will happen to the 144,000? What are the proclamations of the three angels? And what is the "harvest" of Armageddon?

THE LAMB STANDING ON MOUNT ZION

14:1a Then I looked, and behold, a Lamb standing on Mount Zion,

- Chapter 14 is another parenthetical chapter.
- When John the Baptist announced Jesus as the Lamb of God on the banks of Jordan, he introduced Israel to the earthly ministry of Jesus.
- Every time we read of the Lamb in the Book of Revelation, Jesus is always in heaven.
- Pauline and I have visited Mount Zion in Jerusalem many times, but when verse 1 refers to the Lamb standing on Mount Zion, it does not mean Mount Zion in the city of Jerusalem; it refers to Mount Zion in heaven.
- In Romans 11:26, the Bible teaches that Christ will come out of Mount Zion when He returns to deliver the Jewish nation from the hands of the Antichrist at the Battle of Armageddon.

THE 144,000 RAPTURED TO HEAVEN

14:1b and with Him one hundred and forty-four thousand, having His Father's name written on their foreheads.

2 And I heard a voice from heaven, like the voice of many waters, and like the voice of loud thunder. And I heard the sound of harpists playing their harps.

3 They sang as it were a new song before the throne, before the four living creatures, and the elders; and no one could learn that song except the hundred and forty-four thousand who were redeemed from the earth.

4 These are the ones who were not defiled with women, for they are virgins. These are the ones who follow the Lamb wherever He goes. These were redeemed from among men, being firstfruits to God and to the Lamb.

5 And in their mouth was found no deceit, for they are without fault before the throne of God.

- The 144,000 Jewish evangelists were on earth in chapter 7 and they are in heaven in chapter 14.
- The rapture of the manchild in chapter 12:5 symbolizes the rapture of the 144,000.

ADDITIONAL FACTS ABOUT THE 144,000

- They are the only group in the Bible that number 144,000.
- Songs in the Bible are sung because of a special victory or a unique spiritual experience.
- The fact that they alone can sing their song suggests that their experience was unique to them.
- They were the first to be raptured after the Rapture of the church.
- They were the only people to be raptured who lived in one generation. For example when the church is raptured, Old Testament saints together with people who are alive at the time of the Rapture will be caught up together.
- The 144,000 were all saved, all sealed, all commissioned to preach and all raptured within the first three and a half years of the seven year tribulation.

- They were the only company of redeemed in this book that were all Jews.
- They are the only people who will see God's judgment fall on others, but they themselves will be protected.
- They were the only company in the book of Revelation who were sealed by an angel.
- They were the only people who had the Father's Name written on their foreheads.
- With so many unique experiences on earth it is no wonder they were around God's throne in heaven and sang a new song that no one else could sing.
- The sound of their praise was like the sound of many waters and like the voice of loud thunder.
- They were included in the multitudes of people who were redeemed from the earth.
- The redeemed from the earth would include all the saints of earth who are now in heaven.
- The Bible states that they were pure and had not become involved with idolatry or the religious system.
- They were totally committed to Christ.
- They are called the first fruits to God and to the Lamb. This means that they were the first group of people to be raptured during the seven year tribulation.
- The church was raptured before the tribulation.
- They proclaimed the truth and were without fault before God.

THE PROCLAMATION OF THE FIRST ANGEL

14:6 Then I saw another angel flying in the midst of heaven, having the everlasting gospel to preach to those who dwell on the earth—to every nation, tribe, tongue, and people—
7 saying with a loud voice, "Fear God and give glory to Him, for the hour of His judgment has come; and worship Him who made heaven and earth, the sea and springs of water."

- This is the first of three angels that fly in the heavens preaching the everlasting gospel.
- The everlasting gospel is the same gospel we are commissioned to preach today. The only difference is that we warn men that judgment is coming while the angel warns men that God's judgment has arrived.
- The angel flies low in the heavens so that his message can be heard by the people on earth.

THE ANGEL'S MESSAGE

- Fear God.
- Give glory to Him for the hour of His judgment has come.
- Worship Him who made heaven and earth, the sea and springs of water.
- This message will be proclaimed after the Antichrist and the False Prophet are introduced as the two beasts who deceive men by the miracles they were able to perform.
- Although the people on earth have rejected all of God's calls, God in His grace and mercy commissions three angels to preach the Gospel.
- They call men to fear God, escape His judgment, not to worship the Antichrist, but worship the Creator of the universe.

THE PROCLAMATION OF THE SECOND ANGEL

14:8 And another angel followed, saying, "Babylon is fallen, is fallen, that great city, because she has made all nations drink of the wine of the wrath of her fornication."
- The message of the second angel proclaims that the city of Babylon is fallen.
- Babylon will be destroyed at the end of the tribulation under the seventh bowl of judgment.

- Some have reported that Iraq will eventually have its capital in the rebuilt city of Babylon. It is currently being restored with financial aid from the U. S. Government according to the independent military publication *Stars and Stripes*, June 28, 2009 (www.stripes.com).
- It has been reported that 250,000 are already living in rebuilt Babylon. Many speculate that the new city will become a center of commerce, industry, and finance.
- This confirms what the Book of Revelation predicts.
- Other reports state that Suddam Hussein had his initials inscribed on every stone in the rebuilding of the city (during his reign) while Nebuchadnezzar had his name engraved on one stone out of every 100 stones.
- Islamic tradition teaches that in the end time Iraq and Syria will unite as one nation.

THE PROCLAMATION OF THE THIRD ANGEL

14:9 Then a third angel followed them, saying with a loud voice, "If anyone worships the beast and his image, and receives his mark on his forehead or on his hand,

10 he himself shall also drink of the wine of the wrath of God, which is poured out full strength into the cup of His indignation. He shall be tormented with fire and brimstone in the presence of the holy angels and in the presence of the Lamb.

11 And the smoke of their torment ascends forever and ever; and they have no rest day or night, who worship the beast and his image, and whoever receives the mark of his name."

- The third angel's message is a stern warning to the following people who worship the Antichrist.
- People who take the mark of the beast in their foreheads or in their right hand.

- The penalty will be that they will drink of the wine of the wrath (righteous anger) of God.
- These verses prove that hell is eternal.
- These verses speak of punishment to those who refuse to heed the above warnings.
- They will be tormented with fire and brimstone in the presence of the holy angels and in the presence of the Lamb.
- The smoke of their torment ascends for ever and ever.
- They have no rest day or night.
- God promises hell and eternal torment to those who accept the mark of the beast and reject the Lord Jesus Christ.
- God's commissioning of the three angels is His final act of love in the seven year tribulation.

PATIENCE OF THE SAINTS

14:12 Here is the patience of the saints; here are those who keep the commandments of God and the faith of Jesus.
13 Then I heard a voice from heaven saying to me, "Write: 'Blessed are the dead who die in the Lord from now on.'" "Yes," says the Spirit, "that they may rest from their labors, and their works follow them."
- In Revelation 6:9-11, the people who had been killed as martyrs were told to rest until the remaining martyrs would be killed.
- In these verses they are encouraged to rest from their labors and their works follow them.
- The tribulation martyrs are mentioned one more time during the seven year tribulation and that is in chapter 15 verses 2-4.
- They are in heaven and the final time we read of the tribulation martyrs is in chapter 20 verse 4 when they are living on the earth and reigning with Christ over the sheep nations during the Millennium.
- John hears a voice from heaven saying, *Blessed are the dead who die in the Lord from now on. They may rest from the labors.*

- Their works follow them.
- Again, John is commissioned to write the Book of Revelation.
- There are 16 such references in this book.

ARMAGEDDON—REAPING THE HARVEST

14:14 Then I looked, and behold, a white cloud, and on the cloud sat One like the Son of Man, having on His head a golden crown, and in His hand a sharp sickle.

15 And another angel came out of the temple, crying with a loud voice to Him who sat on the cloud, "Thrust in Your sickle and reap, for the time has come for You to reap, for the harvest of the earth is ripe."

16 So He who sat on the cloud thrust in His sickle on the earth, and the earth was reaped.

- After the three angels fly through heaven, the scene changes.
- John saw Christ sitting on a white cloud.
- He was wearing a golden crown.
- In His hand was a sharp sickle.
- Another angel came out of the temple in heaven and cried with a loud voice to Jesus sitting on the white cloud.
- He said, thrust in your sickle and reap for the time has come for You to reap, for the harvest of the earth is ripe.
- Jesus responded and thrust in His sickle on the earth and the earth was reaped.
- This harvest is the introduction to the Battle of Armageddon.
- The harvest will be reaped after the fall of Babylon, the capitol city of the Antichrist's kingdom.
- The sharp sickle was also mentioned by Joel when he described the destruction of the armies of Armageddon (Joel 3:13).
- The expression, "the time has come for you to reap" suggests that Christ has delayed His judgment until the Battle of Armageddon.

THE HARVEST IS THE BATTLE OF ARMAGEDDON

- As we learned above, the harvest refers to the coming Battle of Armageddon which concludes the seven year tribulation and brings Jesus back to earth to establish His Kingdom.
- Read verses 15 and 16 again and compare the following additional Scriptures in Joel 3:9,13,16.
- Proclaim this among the nations: Prepare for war! Wake up the mighty men, let all the men of war draw near.
- Put in the sickle, for the harvest is ripe. Come, go down for the winepress is full; the vats overflow—for their wickedness is great. The Lord also will roar from Zion and utter His voice from Jerusalem. The heavens and the earth shall shake.
- These additional verses refer to the Second Coming of Christ to fight against the Antichrist and his armies at the Battle of Armageddon.

ARMAGEDDON—REAPING THE GRAPES OF WRATH

14:17 Then another angel came out of the temple which is in heaven, he also having a sharp sickle.

18 And another angel came out from the altar, who had power over fire, and he cried with a loud cry to him who had the sharp sickle, saying, "Thrust in your sharp sickle and gather the clusters of the vine of the earth, for her grapes are fully ripe."

19 the angel thrust his sickle into the earth and gathered the vine of the earth, and threw it into the great winepress of the wrath of God.

20 And the winepress was trampled outside the city, and blood came out of the winepress, up to the horses' bridles, for one thousand six hundred furlongs.

- This is another picture of the Battle of Armageddon.

- A second angel with a sharp sickle comes out of the heavenly temple.
- Another angel comes from the altar.
- This angel has power over fire and commands the angel with the sickle to gather the cluster of grapes and place them in the winepress of God's anger.
- The Bible states that the Battle of Armageddon will be fought outside the city, or outside the city of Jerusalem.
- Pauline and I have stood on the very spot where the Battle of Armageddon will be fought.
- It is an area of 100 square miles.
- When Napoleon first visited there he said, "What a great place for a battle." Did he know that he was speaking prophetically?
- The Book of Revelation predicts that blood will flow up to the horses' bridles for about 184 miles (chapter 14:20).

CHRIST TREADING THE WINEPRESS OF HIS ANGER

- The following Scriptures also refer to Christ treading the winepress of His anger at His Second Coming:
- Revelation 19:15: "He Himself treads the winepress of the fierceness and wrath of Almighty God"
- Isaiah 63:2-3: "Why is your apparel red, and your garments like one who treads in the winepress? I have trodden the winepress alone...I have trodden them in my anger, and trampled them in my fury."
- It will take seven months to bury the dead and seven years to destroy the weapons of war (Ezekiel 39:8-16).

REVELATION:
CHAPTER FIFTEEN

Here, we learn about the sea of glass and how the Temple in heaven is opened once again.

PREPARATION FOR THE
SEVEN BOWLS OF JUDGMENTS

15:1 Then I saw another sign in heaven, great and marvelous: seven angels having the seven last plagues, for in them the wrath of God is complete.

- In chapter 6, we outlined the seven seals of judgment.
- In chapters 8 through 11, we outlined the seven trumpets of judgment.
- These judgments occurred during the first half of the seven year tribulation.
- Now in chapter 15, the seven angels prepare to pour out the seven bowls of judgment.
- As with the seven seals of judgment and the seven trumpets of judgment, the seven bowls of judgment occur consecutively.
- The seven bowls of judgment will occur in the last half of the tribulation. They are explained fully in chapter 16.

A PARENTHETICAL CHAPTER

- Chapter 15 is the sixth parenthetical passage in the book of Revelation.
- Verse 1 declares, *"the wrath of God is complete."*

- The word *complete* carries with it the idea that these judgments will bring to an end or finish God's outpoured judgments.
- After the seven bowls of judgment there will be no more.

A SEA OF GLASS

15:2 And I saw something like a sea of glass mingled with fire, and those who have the victory over the beast, over his image and over his mark and over the number of his name, standing on the sea of glass, having harps of God.

3 They sing the song of Moses, the servant of God, and the song of the Lamb, saying:

4 "Who shall not fear You, O Lord, and glorify Your name? For You alone are holy. For all nations shall come and worship before You, For Your judgments have been manifested. Great and marvelous are your works, Lord God Almighty! Just and true are Your ways, O King of the saints."

- We were introduced to the sea of glass in chapter 4.
- At that time the sea of glass was not occupied; here in verse 2 it is crowded with tribulation saints singing songs of victory.
- As you read the rest of verse 3 and verse 4 you read the words of their victory songs.
- The song of Moses was the song Israel sang when they crossed over the Red Sea. It was a song of victory.
- Verse 4 states that *"all nations shall come and worship before You."*
- This will happen when Jesus the King establishes His Kingdom on the earth in the Millennium.
- Those nations who refuse to come to Jerusalem to honor His Royal Majesty, King Jesus, will suffer drought and famine because God will withhold the rain (Zechariah 14:16-19).

THE LAST OF THE MARTYRS ARE IN HEAVEN

- In the fifth seal of judgment (chapter 6: 9-11), the Lord tells the first of the tribulation martyrs that He would wait until all the martyrs had been killed before He judged their enemies.
- We noted in chapter 14 verses 12 and 13 that the martyrs are now blessed in heaven and they have ceased from their labors on earth and their works follow them so that they will be rewarded and assigned a place of authority to rule with Christ in the Millennium.
- We have stated that all the tribulation martyrs would be resurrected and raptured together at the end of the seven year tribulation.
- In John's vision this will occur and the Bride of Christ is complete to celebrate the Marriage Supper of the Lamb.
- In verse 2 through 4 above, all the tribulation martyrs are standing on the sea of glass and are worshiping the Lord.
- Obviously, they have been resurrected and caught up to heaven because the next time we read of them is in chapter 20 verse 4 when they are alive and reigning on earth with Christ for 1,000 years.

THE TEMPLE IN HEAVEN OPENED AGAIN

15:5 After these things I looked, and behold, the temple of the tabernacle of the testimony in heaven was opened.
6 And out of the temple came the seven angels having the seven plagues, clothed in pure bright linen, and having their chests girded with golden bands.
7 Then one of the four living creatures gave to the seven angels seven golden bowls full of the wrath of God who lives forever and ever.

8 The temple was filled with smoke from the glory of God and from His power, and no one was able to enter the temple till the seven plagues of the seven angels were completed.

- The seven angels are preparing to pour out the final seven bowls of judgment.
- Smoke surrounding the glory of God is used ten times in the Book of Revelation and is always associated with judgment.
- This is the second time heaven's temple will be opened.
- This is the final scene in heaven before God's final anger is released and the final seven bowls of judgment are poured out upon the earth.
- One of the living creatures will give the seven golden bowls full of God's wrath to each of the seven angels who will pour them out on the earth.
- The temple will be filled with smoke which comes from the glory of God and from His power.
- Until the angels finish their assignments of judgment, no one was able to enter the temple.

REVELATION:
CHAPTER SIXTEEN

Who are the "seven bowls" of God's judgment? And how do they relate to the Battle of Armageddon? It is explained in this chapter.

ANGELS PREPARE TO POUR OUT THE SEVEN BOWLS OF JUDGMENT

16:1 Then I heard a loud voice from the temple saying to the seven angels, "Go and pour out the bowls of the wrath of God on the earth."

- This verse is still describing what is happening in the temple in heaven in preparation for the bowls of judgment to be poured out on the earth.
- We have examined the seven seals of judgment and the seven trumpets of judgment during the first half of the tribulation.
- Now we will discuss the seven bowls of judgment in the second half of the seven year tribulation.
- These will be God's final judgments which will prepare for the Battle of Armageddon and the Second Coming of Christ.
- They are listed below and we will discuss them one by one.

A LIST OF THE SEVEN BOWLS OF JUDGMENT

- First bowl – loathsome sores inflicted on people.
- Second bowl – the sea turned to blood.

- Third bowl – rivers turned to blood.
- Fourth bowl – scorching heat from the sun.
- Fifth bowl – dense darkness on the Antichrist's kingdom.
- Sixth bowl – the Euphrates river dried up.
- Seventh bowl – a great earthquake and hail weighing 114 lbs falling from heaven.

First Bowl—Loathsome Sores

16:2 So the first went and poured out his bowl upon the earth, and a foul and loathsome sore came upon the men who had the mark of the beast and those who worshiped his image.
- This verse affirms that the tribulation will not be world wide but will affect only the nations which make up the Antichrist's kingdom.
- The foul and loathsome sores will afflict only those who have taken the mark of the beast and those who have worshiped his image.
- This plague is a repeat of one of the plagues God used against Egypt when Pharaoh refused to let Israel go free.

Second Bowl—The Sea Turns to Blood

16:3 Then the second angel poured out his bowl on the sea, and it became blood as of a dead man; and every living creature in the sea died.
- When the second angel poured out the second trumpet judgment in chapter 8 verses 8 and 9, the Bible stated that one-third of the sea became blood and one-third of the fish died.
- Under the second bowl of judgment the Bible states that all the sea became blood and all the fish died.

THIRD BOWL—RIVERS TURN TO BLOOD

16:4 Then the third angel poured out his bowl on the rivers and springs of water, and they became blood.

5 And I heard the angel of the waters saying: "You are righteous, O Lord, The One who is and who was and who is to be, Because You have judged these things.

6 For they have shed the blood of saints and prophets, And You have given them blood to drink. For it is their just due."

7 And I heard another from the altar saying, "Even so, Lord God Almighty, true and righteous are Your judgments."

- In the third trumpet judgment, one-third of the rivers were poisoned (chapter 8:10-11).
- In the plagues of Egypt, the rivers turned to blood. Now, under the third bowl this judgment is repeated.
- These verses affirm that God's judgments fall on those who have shed innocent blood.
- This judgment is followed by angels praising God for His just and righteous judgment in sending these plagues.

FOURTH BOWL—MEN ARE SCORCHED

16:8 Then the fourth angel poured out his bowl on the sun, and power was given to him to scorch men with fire.

9 And men were scorched with great heat, and they blasphemed the name of God who has power over these plagues; and they did not repent and give Him glory.

- In this judgment the fourth angel had power to increase the heat of the sun so that mankind was scorched with great heat.
- People obviously knew that all these judgments came from an angry and a just God, yet instead of these judgments bringing repentance, people blasphemed the name of God— and they did not repent and give Him glory.

169

FIFTH BOWL—DARKNESS AND PAIN

16:10 Then the fifth angel poured out his bowl on the throne of the beast, and his kingdom became full of darkness; and they gnawed their tongues because of the pain.

11 They blasphemed the God of heaven because of their pains and their sores, and did not repent of their deeds.

- This judgment is similar to the ninth Egyptian plague.
- It was poured out on the throne of the beast (the Antichrist), and his kingdom.
- The kingdom of the Antichrist became dark and people gnawed their tongues because of the pain.
- At this time, the Antichrist has set up his throne in the rebuilt temple in Jerusalem.
- Although the pain will be unbearable, people still blasphemed the God of heaven because of their pains and sores, and did not repent of their deeds.
- These verses show the rebellion and unbelief in the hearts of sinful humanity.

SIXTH BOWL—THE RIVER EUPHRATES DRIED UP

16:12 Then the sixth angel poured out his bowl on the great river Euphrates, and its water was dried up, so that the way of the kings from the east might be prepared.

13 And I saw three unclean spirits like frogs coming out of the mouth of the dragon, out of the mouth of the beast, and out of the mouth of the false prophet.

14 For they are spirits of demons, performing signs, which go out to the kings of the earth and of the whole world, to gather them to the battle of that great day of God Almighty.

- These verses reveal the final preparation for the Battle of Armageddon.

• Just as God caused the Red Sea and the river Jordan to dry up, He will cause the river Euphrates to dry up so that the armies from the East might assemble for the Battle of Armageddon.

DEMONS LIKE FROGS ARE SPOKEN WORDS

• John saw three demon spirits that looked like frogs come out of the mouth of the dragon, out of the mouth of the beast (the Antichrist) and out of the mouth of the False Prophet.
• These demons inspired the words of the dragon, the Antichrist, and the False Prophet to influence additional world leaders to join the Antichrist and fight against Christ and the nation of Israel at the Battle of Armageddon.

THE POWER OF WORDS

• Words are not just sounds.
• Jesus said, *"The words that I speak to you are Spirit and they are life"* (John 6:63).
• On the other hand, the words spoken by the Antichrist were spirit and death.
• Several years ago my wife and I were betrayed by a man I trusted as a brother and a friend. He stole all our life's savings and I was an emotional wreck.
• One night, Pauline came into my office and spoke the following words that changed my life: "Roy, do not allow his demons to destroy you. Let the mighty warrior within you rise and do battle."
• Her words broke the mental and emotional chains that had bound me.
• Words are either spirit and life or spirit and death; spirit and health or spirit and sickness; spirit and victory or spirit and defeat; spirit and success or spirit and failure.

- Solomon wrote, "Death and life are in the power of the tongue" (Proverbs 18:21).
- Positive Bible faith confession has been ridiculed and rejected in many church circles, but it is a valid, life changing truth.

THE MISPLACED VERSE IN THE BOOK OF REVELATION

16:15 "Behold, I am coming as a thief. Blessed is he who watches, and keeps his garments, lest he walk naked and they see his shame."
- Some Bible scholars call verse 15 the misplaced verse in the Book of Revelation.
- It would seem to fit better with Christ's letter to the Laodicean church in chapter 3 verses 14-22.
- Some teach that this verse was an illustration taken from the workers in the temple.
- If they were found sleeping in the temple, tradition says that they were stripped and sent from the temple to walk home naked.
- Although they could insist they had not been sleeping on the job, people would see their nakedness and witness their shame.
- Whatever the context, believers are commanded to watch for the coming of Christ and be clothed with the garments of righteousness.
- When Jesus comes He will come as a thief without warning.

THE BATTLE OF ARMAGEDDON

16:16 And they gathered them together to the place called in Hebrew, Armageddon.
- There are many references in the Bible to the Battle of Armageddon, but verse 16 is the only verse that identifies the battle by name.

- It comes from a Greek name "Harmageddon" which means, Mount of Megiddo.
- It is located on the south side of the valley of Megiddo, south west of Mount Carmel.
- The main highway between Asia and Africa runs through the valley and the valley is a key location between the Euphrates and the Nile rivers.
- It has been the site of many battles in past history and it will be the battleground for the final conflict, the Battle of Armageddon, the most violent confrontation in human history.
- Thothmes III, the founder of the ancient Egyptian Empire, when he saw the location of the Battle of Armageddon, said, "Megiddo is worth a thousand cities."
- Throughout history, past and present, many battles have been called by that name but this will be the actual Battle of Armageddon of Bible prophecy.

SEVENTH BOWL— AN EARTHQUAKE AND GREAT HAIL

16:17 Then the seventh angel poured out his bowl into the air, and a loud voice came out of the temple of heaven, from the throne, saying, "It is done!"

18 And there were noises and thunderings and lightnings; and there was a great earthquake, such a mighty and great earthquake as had not occurred since men were on the earth.

19 Now the great city was divided into three parts, and the cities of the nations fell. And great Babylon was remembered before God, to give her the cup of the wine of the fierceness of His wrath.

20 Then every island fled away, and the mountains were not found.

21 And great hail from heaven fell upon men, each hailstone about the weight of a talent. Men blasphemed God because of the plague of the hail, since that plague was exceedingly great.

- The seventh and final bowl of judgment will be the most severe judgment of all.
- Verse 17 states, *It is done.* This means it is over, or the judgments have come to an end.
- First, the world will experience the most devastating and destructive earthquake in history.
- The earthquake will be accompanied by loud noises, thunder and lightning.
- Cities around the world will be reduced to ruins.
- Babylon, which had been the capital of the Antichrist, will be destroyed because of God's fierce anger.
- Islands and mountains will be destroyed or removed.
- In addition to the chaos and confusion of the most destructive earthquake the world has ever known, hailstones weighing up to 114 lbs in weight will fall from heaven.
- All of this will occur, together with the bloodiest battle the world has ever known, the Battle of Armageddon.
- In spite of this final act of God's judgment, men will continue to defy and blaspheme Him.

REVELATION:
CHAPTER SEVENTEEN

In John's vision, he saw "Mystery" Babylon, a deceptive false religion. This chapter also introduces the final kingdom.

THE SCARLET HARLOT
SITTING ON THE SCARLET BEAST

- This is another parenthetical chapter introducing a false, deceptive religious system, which martyred many of the saints of God.
- It is called, Mystery Babylon.
- The harlot.
- The mother of harlots.
- The mother of the abominations of the earth.
- The great whore.
- The great city.

17:1 Then one of the seven angels who had the seven bowls came and talked with me, saying to me, "Come, I will show you the judgment of the great harlot who sits on many waters,
2 with whom the kings of the earth committed fornication, and the inhabitants of the earth were made drunk with the wine of her fornication."
3 So he carried me away in the Spirit into the wilderness. And I saw a woman sitting on a scarlet beast which was full of names of blasphemy, having seven heads and ten horns.

4 The woman was arrayed in purple and scarlet, and adorned with gold and precious stones and pearls, having in her hand a golden cup full of abominations and the filthiness of her fornication.

5 And on her forehead a name was written: MYSTERY, BABYLON THE GREAT, THE MOTHER OF HARLOTS AND OF THE ABOMINATIONS OF THE EARTH.

6 I saw the woman, drunk with the blood of the saints and with the blood of the martyrs of Jesus. And when I saw her, I marveled with great amazement. "The kings of the earth and the inhabitants of the earth were made drunk with the wine of her fornication"

- This religion influenced the ten nation confederation for the first half of the seven year tribulation.
- The fact that she sits on many waters suggests that the religious system has influenced many nations.
- Fornication and playing the harlot in both the Old and New Testaments have always symbolized idolatry and false religions (Isaiah 23:17; 57:3-5; Jeremiah 3:1- 6; Ezekiel 6: 1-17; 20:3-32; 23:7-4; Hosea 4:12-19; Nahum 3:43; James 4:4).

THE BEAST WITH SEVEN HEADS AND TEN HORNS

- In John's vision of the woman, she is riding on a scarlet colored beast with seven heads and ten horns.
- The Bible says the beast was full of names of blasphemy.
- We were introduced to the beast in chapter 13.
- Daniel 7 also refers to the beast with ten horns.
- The seven heads refer to the seven world empires that have persecuted Israel in past history.
- We have learned that they are Egypt, Assyria, Babylon, Medes and Persians, Greece, Rome.
- The ten horns are ten nations of revised Rome which will be the seventh world power.

- When the ten nations are totally controlled by the Antichrist, they will become the eighth world power and will be destroyed together with other nations at the Battle of Armageddon when Christ returns.
- This religious system will dominate and control the ten nation confederation for the first three and a half years until she is destroyed by the Antichrist, the False Prophet and the ten nations in the middle of the seven year tribulation (chapter 17: 9-17).

THE WEALTH OF THE RELIGIOUS SYSTEM

- The dress and the jewelry of the Great Whore represent her great wealth.
- Her dress was purple and red.
- Her jewelry was gold, precious stones and pearls.
- She holds a golden cup full of abominations and the filthiness of her fornication.
- Thus, she had seduced many nations with her false religion and had influenced them to reject the true God and follow her apostate, false religious doctrine.
- Her name is significant: MYSTERY BABYLON THE GREAT. THE MOTHER OF HARLOTS AND OF THE ABOMINATIONS OF THE EARTH.
- Mystery Babylon, the mother of harlots suggests that it is connected to the ancient mysterious religion of Babylon.
- This cult was characterized by the word, MYSTERY.

THE ANCIENT BABYLONIAN RELIGION

- The ancient Babylonian religion was founded by Nimrod and his queen, Semiramis (Genesis 11).

- It quickly spread among all peoples of that day because every one spoke the same language and national boundaries had not yet been established.
- Nimrod built cities with walls to prevent men from being attacked by wild animals.
- He taught men to reject a holy God who was angry at sin.
- He influenced the people to build the tower of Babel which, he said, would reach to heaven.
- The tower of Babel was a blasphemous attempt to defy God.
- Nimrod's wife, Semiranis was an object of worship.
- She was a woman of unbridled lust and immoral behavior.
- She was called the mother of all impurity.
- She sanctified prostitution to her pagan gods.

MYSTICAL BABYLON AND THE CATHOLIC CHURCH

Some readers may misinterpret my comments regarding the false religion and the Roman Catholic Church. I have preached in several Roman Catholic churches, cathedrals, and leadership seminars around the world. I was given a special dispensation of grace to participate in the Mass. Several years ago I teamed up in ministry with a Cardinal who was a personal representative of the Pope.

But many scholars, including Catholic scholars believe the false religion of chapter 13 will be the Roman Catholic Church.

- In 1825, Pope Leo XII had a medal with his image on one side and a woman on the other side.
- The woman held a cross in one hand and a cup in her right hand.
- She represented the Roman Catholic Church.
- On the medal were inscribed the words in Latin, which would be translated, "The whole world is her seat."

- According to Hislop's, *The Two Babylons*, with research from 260 sources, we learn the following interesting facts about this ancient religion:
- The tower of Babel was built as a monument to that religion.
- The objects of worship were the supreme Father, the incarnate queen of heaven and her son.
- Actually worship was focused mostly on the heavenly queen mother and her son.
- The cult claimed the highest mystical wisdom and professed to know the most sacred mysteries.
- They had confession to priests.
- Without confession no one could take the sacrament.
- They practiced many mysterious religious rites.
- The rosary was used for prayer.
- Julius Caesar became the head of the Roman branch of the Babylonian cult in 63 B.C.
- Other Roman Emperors held the office until 376 A.D.
- In 376 A.D. the Emperor Gratian, who was a converted Christian, refused the office because he saw the idolatry of the ancient religious cult.
- Damasus, Bishop of the Christian church at Rome was elected to the office in 378 A.D.
- From that time this Babylonian religious cult has increasingly influenced the Roman Catholic Church.
- Temples, cathedrals and ornate church buildings were built and the religious rites of heathen temples were introduced.
- Worshiping images, idols and the veneration of saints became the practice of the church.
- Worship of the Virgin Mary started three years after Damasus become the leader of this religious cult.
- Worshiping Mary as the mother of God and her Son is a carry over of the Babylonian religion worshiping the Queen of heaven and her son.

- Private confessions and penance were introduced.
- Scourgings, pilgrimages and making the sign of the cross were practiced.
- Christmas, Our Lady Day, Easter, Lent, and other pagan religious festival were introduced.
- Once people were admitted to this religious cult, they no longer referred to their original nationality, they became a member of a mystical brotherhood, over whom was placed a Supreme Pontiff whose word was final in their lives, regardless of their national citizenship.
- The order of monks and nuns is of Babylonian origin.
- The above statements have influenced people to believe that this false and deceptive religion which influenced the ten nations of the Antichrist is the Roman Catholic Church.
- Even several Roman Catholic scholars believe that Revelation 17 describes their church. These include Pope Pius X, St. Vincent, St. Francis, Father O'Conner, Cardinal Ballarmine, the French Prelate, Boussuet, and Bishop Sheen, who was very popular on television a few years ago.
- Cardinal Newman in his book, *The Development of the Christian Church*, writes that Temples, incense, oil lamps, votive offerings, Holy water, holidays and seasons of devotions, processions, blessings of fields, sacerdotal vestments, the tonsure of priests, monks and nuns and images are all of pagan origin.
- Verse 6 describes that this religious system is responsible for the blood of the martyrs.
- Other scholars believe that this apostate church will be a worldwide ecumenical church, led by the Roman Catholic Church and will include liberal Protestant churches.

MYSTICAL BABYLON AND THE FUTURE RELIGIOUS SYSTEM

- In spite of the evidence that the religious system which dominates the ten nations is Roman Catholicism, I cannot believe that the five Middle Eastern nations who follow the Islamic religion could accept the Roman Catholic teachings as they are taught today.
- I believe that the Apostate Pope, as the False Prophet, will use deceptive visions of the Virgin Mary and his ability to perform miracles to present a perverted doctrine of the ancient Babylonian cult that is acceptable to an apostate Roman Catholic Church and a perverted Islamic faith.
- Obviously the false religion must be accepted by both Roman Catholics and Muslims.

ADDITIONAL TRUTH ABOUT THE WOMAN AND THE BEAST

17:7 But the angel said to me, "Why did you marvel? I will tell you the mystery of the woman and of the beast that carries her, which has the seven heads and the ten horns.
- In the vision John saw the beast carrying the woman; therefore they must be two different identities.
- As we have explained the beast is the kingdom ruled by the Antichrist and the woman is Mystery Babylon, a false religious system which is supported by the Antichrist, by the False Prophet and by the kingdom of the Antichrist until the middle of the seven year tribulation.

THE MEANING OF THE BEAST

17:8 The beast that you saw was, and is not, and will ascend out of the bottomless pit and go to perdition. And those who

181

dwell on the earth will marvel, whose names are not written in the Book of Life from the foundation of the world, when they see the beast that was, and is not, and yet is.

- The beast represents three things.
    - (1) A fallen angel that comes up out of the bottomless pit to empower and orchestrate everything that happens to the Antichrist and by the Antichrist.
    - (2) The Antichrist himself who is satanically inspired.
    - (3) The kingdom of the Antichrist which is orchestrated by the fallen angel.
- The beast (the kingdom) John saw "was" (in past history), "and is not" (during John's time) "and will ascend out of the bottomless pit."
- In other words, the kingdom was prominent in past history; it did not exist as a world power during John's day, but will become a super power again as the eighth kingdom ruled by the Antichrist.
- This will be the final world power before Christ returns to fight at the Battle of Armageddon and establish His world wide Kingdom on earth with Jerusalem as His world capital.

The Seven Heads and Seven Mountains Are Seven Kingdoms

17:9 "Here is the mind which has wisdom: The seven heads are seven mountains on which the woman sits.
10 There (these are or they are) are also seven kings (or seven kingdoms). Five have fallen, one is, and the other has not yet come. And when he comes, he must continue a short time."

- The words kings and kingdoms are used interchangeably in Scripture.
- We have discussed the six world powers of past history.

- Some prophecy preachers teach that the five kings that have fallen, are five Roman emperors and the sixth was Domitan who ruled the empire during John's day. They believe that the seventh head represents the Antichrist and the eighth kingdom is the Antichrist raised from the dead.
- I reject the above interpretation.
- The seventh world power will be the ten nation confederation which did not have full political and military power until they were formed and the Antichrist came from one of them.
- The Antichrist will defeat three of the ten nations and the other nations will accept him as their absolute leader.
- Once the ten nations accept the Antichrist as their leader, they will become the eighth world power.
- They will fight against Christ at the Battle of Armageddon and be destroyed when Jesus Christ returns.
- The seven mountains on which the woman sits have also been the source of much controversy as we shall see below.
- Some scholars have translated the seven mountains as seven hills and because Rome is called the city on the seven hills, many have concluded that this referred to Rome.
- The correct translation should read. The seven heads are seven mountains on which the woman sits. They (the seven heads and the seven mountains) are (symbolize) seven kingdoms.
- In other words the seven mountains symbolize the seven kingdoms of Egypt, Assyria, Babylon, Medes and Persia, Greece, Rome and the ten nations which will come from the Revised Roman Empire.
- If the seven mountains refer to the seven hills on which Rome sits, five of the hills must have disappeared, one hill remains and another hill is yet to come. How foolish!
- The five kingdoms that had fallen were, Egypt, Assyria, Babylon, Medes and Persians and Greece.
- The kingdom that is during John's day was the Empire of Rome.

- The kingdom that had not yet come will be the ten nation confederation which will be formed within the boundary of the former Roman Empire.
- The Bible says, He must continue a short time.
- Actually, the ten nation confederation will last only three and a half years.
- The eighth and final kingdom will be introduced in verse 11.
- That is when the Antichrist is revealed as the beast, breaks his peace pact with Israel, destroys the religious system, rules over the ten nations as the eighth world power and attempts to destroy Israel.
- This will lead to the Battle of Armageddon.

THE EIGHTH AND FINAL KINGDOM IS INTRODUCED

17:11 The beast that was, and is not, is himself also the eighth, and is of the seven, and is going to perdition.

12 "The ten horns which you saw are ten kings who have received no kingdom as yet, but they receive authority for one hour as kings with the beast.

13 These are of one mind, and they will give their power and authority to the beast.

- The beast (kingdom) "that was and is not" is also the eighth and is one of the seven.
- This teaches that the eighth and final kingdom was a powerful kingdom in past history and was not in power during John's day.
- That eliminates Rome.
- Verses 11 and 12 teach that the ten horns, or ten kingdoms, had limited authority as a world power until the Antichrist became their leader and their position as a world power will be brief.

THE EIGHTH AND FINAL KINGDOM IS IDENTIFIED

- Some teach that the eighth kingdom under Antichrist for the final three and a half years will be a revised Rome because the ten nations will originally be formed within the boundaries of the Roman Empire. We have proved above that it cannot be Rome.
- Some teach that it will be a revival of the former Assyrian Empire because the Antichrist is called the Assyrian and he will come from Syria.
- Others teach that it will be revived Babylon because the Antichrist will make his headquarters in the city of Babylon during the tribulation and he is called the king of Babylon.
- I believe it will be revived Greece for the following reasons:
- In Daniel chapter 8 the Bible identifies the goat as Greece.
- The Bible predicted that when the first king of Greece died, the Empire would be divided into four divisions and the little horn (the Antichrist) would come from one of the four divisions.
- Alexander was the first leader of Greece and history confirms the accuracy of Bible prophecy.
- At Alexander's death, the Empire was divided into four divisions and assigned to four generals.
- Those divisions would be known today as Greece, Turkey, Syria and Egypt.
- Because the little horn, the Antichrist, will come from the former Grecian Empire, it is a clear sign that revived Greece will have to be the eighth kingdom.
- This is what the angel meant in verse 8 when he said, the beast (kingdom) was (in past history) and is not (during John's day) and shall ascend out of the bottomless pit to become the eighth kingdom under Antichrist and shall go to perdition.
- The spirit that shall ascend out of the bottomless pit is the spirit of ancient Greece.

185

- God's angel who visited Daniel had to fight the ruling prince (the ruling spirit) of Greece (Daniel 10:20).
- Revelation 17:8 concludes with the beast "that was and is not and yet is" confirms the same truth, the kingdom of Greece *was* in past history and *is not* in John's day and *yet is* in John's prophetic vision of the future.
- Many Bible scholars who believe that the Antichrist will come from Syria also believe that the three nations he will conquer will be the other three divisions of the ancient Greek Empire, namely Greece, Turkey, and Egypt.
- In Revelation 13:2 the body of the beast (the Antichrist) was the body of a leopard, which in Daniel 7 symbolized Greece.
- In Joel 3:6 and Zechariah 9:13 there are prophecies of the Grecian Empire under the control of the Antichrist.
- Daniel 11 deals with the past history and the future prophecy of Egypt and Syria.
- Egypt was the southern division and Syria was the northern division.
- These two nations fought bloody battles for many years.
- In verse 36 the chapter moves from history to prophecy and predicts that in the end time, the leader of the northern division of the two nations, namely Syria, will become the Antichrist and will defeat Egypt.
- This proves that the eighth kingdom will be the final empire of the Antichrist.

ARMAGEDDON—A CLASH
BETWEEN TWO KINGDOMS

17:14 These will make war with the Lamb, and the Lamb will overcome them, for He is Lord of lords and King of kings; and those who are with Him are called, chosen, and faithful."

- As we have learned, the Battle of Armageddon began as a battle between nations.
- Now it becomes a clash between the conflicting kingdoms— The Kingdom of Light and the kingdom of darkness.

15 Then he said to me, "The waters which you saw, where the harlot sits, are peoples, multitudes, nations, and tongues."
- The false religion, Mystical Babylon influenced multitudes, nations and tongues.

THE HARLOT IS DESTROYED

17:16 And the ten horns which you saw on the beast, these will hate the harlot, make her desolate and naked, eat her flesh and burn her with fire.
- When the Harlot, the religious system was first introduced, the beast carried her.
- In other words, the false, apostate religious system was totally supported by the Antichrist, the False Prophet, and the ten nation confederation over which the Antichrist would rule.
- When the Antichrist gained total control over the ten nations (the ten horns), the Antichrist, the False Prophet and the ten nation confederation turned against the religious system and the Bible says, these will hate the harlot, make her desolate and naked, eat her flesh and burn her with fire.

THE TEN NATIONS UNDER THE ANTICHRIST ARE UNITED

17:17 For God has put it into their hearts to fulfill His purpose, to be of one mind, and to give their kingdom to the beast, until the words of God are fulfilled.
- No matter what happens in the world, historically, politically, financially, culturally, commercially or in any other way, we must know that God is always in control.

- The Antichrist received his power and authority from the dragon, but God orchestrated the whole plan to fulfill His divine purpose.

A FINAL WORD ABOUT THE HARLOT

17:18 And the woman whom you saw is that great city which reigns over the kings of the earth."

- Many scholars believe the great city refers to Rome because they hold that the False Prophet will be a reprobate Pope, who will use his power from Rome to unify the Muslims and apostate Christianity and thus use this false religion to influence the kings of the earth.
- While many scholars believe the great city is Rome, others believe it refers to Babylon (chapters 16:9 and 18:2).
- Babylon is also called "the great city."
- As we have emphasized several times, Babylon will be the headquarters city for the Antichrist during the tribulation.
- Still others nominate New York and London.
- One writer said it was Jerusalem.
- Why can't we believe that Babylon means Babylon, a city on the banks of the Euphrates river?

Revelation:
Chapter Eighteen

God brings total destruction to the Antichrist's capital—and heaven rejoices!

The Fall of the City of Babylon

18:1 After these things I saw another angel coming down from heaven, having great authority, and the earth was illuminated with his glory.

2 And he cried mightily with a loud voice, saying, "Babylon the great is fallen, is fallen, and has become a dwelling place of demons, a prison for every foul spirit, and a cage for every unclean and hated bird!

3 For all the nations have drunk of the wine of the wrath of her fornication, the kings of the earth have committed fornication with her, and the merchants of the earth have become rich through the abundance of her luxury."

4 And I heard another voice from heaven saying, "Come out of her, my people, lest you share in her sins, and lest you receive of her plagues.

Mystical Babylon, a Religion, and the City of Religion

• In chapter 17, we were introduced to Mystery Babylon, a false, deceptive religion.

- In chapter 18, we read of the city of Babylon, the headquarters city of the Antichrist.
- We must keep the city of Babylon and the religion of Babylon separate.
- Study the distinctions below:
- Chapter 17 deals with Mystical Babylon, a religious system; chapter 18 deals with the actual city of Babylon.
- The harlot in chapter 17 is symbolic; the city in chapter 18 is literal.
- Man destroys the religious system of Babylon in chapter 17; God destroys the city of Babylon in chapter 18.
- The religious system of chapter 17 is made rich by deceiving men; the city of Babylon makes others rich by business and commerce.
- Man rejoices over the destruction of the religious system of chapter 17; man laments over the destruction of the city in chapter 18.
- No commerce is mentioned in the activities of the religious system of chapter 17; much commerce is mentioned in the city of Babylon in chapter 18.
- The religious system in chapter 17 is called a harlot; the city of Babylon in chapter 18 is not.
- Names are written on the forehead of the woman, the false religion; no names are written on the city.
- John wonders over the woman (the religious system) but does not wonder over the city.
- Business and trade are not mentioned in the religious system, but are found in the city.
- The Antichrist and the ten nations will rejoice over the destruction of the religious system, but they will mourn over the destruction of the city.

Babylon, the Antichrist's Capital

- The Antichrist will rule from the city of Babylon.

- The ancient city covered 196 square miles.
- On the eastern and western side of the city there were two beautiful palaces that were connected by a bridge almost 1,200 feet long and 30 feet wide.
- There were three huge walls protecting the two palaces.
- The city of Babylon will be destroyed by Christ when He returns at the Battle of Armageddon.
- As we have learned, in addition to his reigning from the city of Babylon, in the final three and a half years of the seven year tribulation, the Antichrist will also set up his religious headquarters in the rebuilt temple in Jerusalem.
- Some scholars believe that according to Jeremiah 51:64, the city of Babylon can never be rebuilt.
- Other scholars believe that this will be true only of the future Babylon after it is destroyed at the Second Coming of Christ.
- Isaiah chapter 13 teaches that Babylon will be destroyed in the future Day of the Lord.
- There are many Scriptures in the Book of Revelation alone which teach that the city of Babylon will be rebuilt.

THE INFLUENCE OF THE CITY OF BABYLON

- Jerusalem was a powerful city in King David's time.
- Rome was a powerful city when Jesus was born.
- London was a powerful city when the British Empire ruled the waves.
- Washington is the most influential city today.
- When the Antichrist comes to power and makes the city of Babylon his headquarters, Babylon will become the most prominent, the most influential and the most important city in the world.
- The Antichrist will lead the world's greatest political, financial, industrial and military might and the city of Babylon will be his capital.

- The Antichrist is killed and the city of Babylon will be destroyed at the Battle of Armageddon at the coming of Jesus Christ.

ADDITIONAL FACTS ABOUT THE CITY OF BABYLON

- God Himself will judge and destroy the city (verse 8).
- Babylon was the site of man's first rebellion against God when man tried to build the tower of Babel and it will be the site of man's last rebellion (chapters 14:8; 16:17- 21; 18:1- 24).
- Babylon has been associated with false religions, idolatry and demon spirits in Scripture (Isaiah 21:9; 47:9-10; Revelation. 18:2-3, 23).
- In verse 4, God commands the tribulation saints to come out of Babylon before judgment falls.
- When the Antichrist establishes his headquarters in the city of Babylon, the city will be a dwelling place for demons, a prison for every foul spirit and a cage for every unclean and hated bird.
- According to Matthew 13:4, 19, these hateful birds are symbolic of demons or unclean spirits.
- Verse 3 teaches that the city of Babylon will persecute the nations that do not accept the false religion, described in chapter 17.
- Those nations who do business with the Antichrist will become rich.

GOD'S JUDGMENT ON THE CITY OF BABYLON

18:5 For her sins have reached to heaven, and God has remembered her iniquities.
6 Render to her just as she rendered to you, and repay her double according to her works; in the cup which she has

mixed, mix double for her.

7 In the measure that she glorified herself and lived luxuriously, in the same measure give her torment and sorrow; for she says in her heart, 'I sit as queen, and am no widow, and will not see sorrow.'

8 Therefore her plagues will come in one day—death and mourning and famine. And she will be utterly burned with fire, for strong is the Lord God who judges her.

- God is a just God. He will reward the righteous and punish the wicked.
- The judgment He will pour out on Babylon will be double because of the following sins committed by the occupants of the city:
- Her pride.
- Her rebellion.
- Her total depravity.
- The religion deception she used on many people.

THE FOURFOLD JUDGMENTS

- The Bible teaches that God's judgments on Babylon are fourfold and will come in one day.
- They include, death, mourning, famine and destruction by fire.

NATIONS MOURN THE FALL OF THE CITY OF BABYLON

18:9 "The kings of the earth who committed fornication and lived luxuriously with her will weep and lament for her, when they see the smoke of her burning,

10 standing at a distance for fear of her torment, saying, 'Alas, alas, that great city Babylon, that mighty city! For in one hour your judgment has come.'

11 And the merchants of the earth will weep and mourn over her, for no one buys their merchandise anymore:

• The nations of the earth that had been influenced by the false religion promoted by the city of Babylon, together with those nations who had been a trade partner with her and the nations under the Antichrist's control, will lament at her destruction.

THE COMMERCIAL BUSINESS OF THE CITY OF BABYLON

18:12 merchandise of gold and silver, precious stones and pearls, fine linen and purple, silk and scarlet, every kind of citron wood, every kind of object of ivory, every kind of object of most precious wood, bronze, iron, and marble;

13 and cinnamon and incense, fragrant oil and frankincense, wine and oil, fine flour and wheat, cattle and sheep, horses and chariots, and bodies and souls of men.

14 The fruit that your soul longed for has gone from you, and all the things which are rich and splendid have gone from you, and you shall find them no more at all.

15 The merchants of these things, who became rich by her, will stand at a distance for fear of her torment, weeping and wailing,

16 and saying, 'Alas, alas, that great city that was clothed in fine linen, purple, and scarlet, and adorned with gold and precious stones and pearls!

17 For in one hour such great riches came to nothing.' Every shipmaster, all who travel by ship, sailors, and as many as trade on the sea, stood at a distance

18 and cried out when they saw the smoke of her burning, saying, 'What is like this great city?'

19 "They threw dust on their heads and cried out, weeping and wailing, and saying, 'Alas, alas, that great city, in which all who had ships on the sea became rich by her wealth! For in one hour she is made desolate.'"

- The Bible mentions the wealth of the city of Babylon.
- Those nations who traded with her also became rich.
- The business trade of Babylon included, gold, silver, precious stones, pearls, purple, scarlet, all kinds of perfumes, wine, oil, wheat, animals, silk, ivory, objects of expensive wood, brass, iron, marble, chariots (automobiles in our day) and human trafficking and slavery.

HEAVEN REJOICES OVER THE DESTRUCTION OF BABYLON

18:20 "Rejoice over her, O heaven, and you holy apostles and prophets, for God has avenged you on her!"
- While there is weeping on earth because of Babylon's destruction, there is rejoicing in heaven.
- The following three times in the Book of Revelation, heaven is told to rejoice:
    1. When Satan was cast down to the earth (chapter 12:12).
    2. When the city of Babylon is destroyed (chapter 18:20).
    3. At the Marriage Supper of the Lamb (chapter 19:7).

THE REASON FOR BABYLON'S TOTAL DESTRUCTION

18:21 Then a mighty angel took up a stone like a great millstone and threw it into the sea, saying, "Thus with violence the great city Babylon shall be thrown down, and shall not be found anymore.
22 The sound of harpists, musicians, flutists, and trumpeters shall not be heard in you anymore. No craftsman of any craft shall be found in you anymore, and the sound of a millstone shall not be heard in you anymore.
23 The light of a lamp shall not shine in you anymore, and the voice of bridegroom and bride shall not be heard in

you anymore. For your merchants were the great men of the earth, for by your sorcery all the nations were deceived. 24 And in her was found the blood of prophets and saints, and of all who were slain on the earth."

- The reason for God's judgment on Babylon was, religious deception, occult activity, idolatry and martyrdom.

THE VIOLENT DESTRUCTION OF BABYLON

- To illustrate the sudden, violent destruction of the city of Babylon, an angel threw a great millstone into the sea.
- Its destruction will mean that, no music will ever be heard in the city again.
- No work will ever be performed in the city again.
- No light will ever be seen in the city again.
- No one will ever get married in the city again.
- Family life in the city will cease.
- There will be a few more verses in the next chapter to describe the climax of the Battle of Armageddon (chapter 19:15-21).

Revelation:
Chapter Nineteen

This chapter describes the amazing events surrounding the Marriage Supper of the Lamb and the Second Coming of Christ.

Rejoicing in Heaven in Preparation for a Wedding

19:1 After these things I heard a loud voice of a great multitude in heaven, saying, "Alleluia! Salvation and glory and honor and power belong to the Lord our God!
- After these things: After the destruction of Mystical Babylon, the false religion in Revelation 17 and the destruction of the city of Babylon at the Battle of Armageddon in Revelation 18, heaven is preparing for the wedding celebration of Christ and His Bride.
- The loud voice of a great multitude. The bride is made up of the redeemed of all ages and they are all in heaven.

More Praise and Worship in Heaven

19:2 For true and righteous are His judgments, because He has judged the great harlot who corrupted the earth with her fornication; and He has avenged on her the blood of His servants shed by her."
3 Again they said, "Alleluia! Her smoke rises up forever and ever!"

4 And the twenty-four elders and the four living creatures fell down and worshiped God who sat on the throne, saying, "Amen! Alleluia!"

- The redeemed sing praises to God in a loud voice because He had judged the great harlot (the false religion) in truth and righteousness and has avenged the blood of the many martyrs who had been killed by her.
- The true bride of Christ, a chaste virgin, is heaven's answer to the great harlot of chapter 17.

THE LAST OF THE MARTYRS IN HEAVEN

- During the fifth seal in chapter 6, the martyrs in heaven asked Jesus how long it would be before He judged the people who had killed them.
- He replied that He would wait until other martyrs would be killed before judgment.
- Now, the last person had been martyred and was in heaven. It is now time for judgment.

THE TWENTY-FOUR ELDERS

- This is the last time we read of the 24 Elders and the four living, angelic creatures in the Book of Revelation.
- We have learned that the 24 elders symbolize the saints of God of all ages.
- The 12 tribes of Israel represent the Old Testament saints.
- The 12 Apostles of the Lamb represent the New Testament saints.

PREPARATION FOR THE MARRIAGE CELEBRATION

19:5 Then a voice came from the throne, saying, "Praise our God, all you His servants and those who fear Him, both small and great!"

6 And I heard, as it were, the voice of a great multitude, as the sound of many waters and as the sound of mighty thunderings, saying, "Alleluia! For the Lord God Omnipotent reigns!

7 Let us be glad and rejoice and give Him glory, for the marriage of the Lamb has come, and His wife has made herself ready."

8 And to her it was granted to be arrayed in fine linen, clean and bright, for the fine linen is the righteous acts of the saints.

9 Then he said to me, "Write: 'Blessed are those who are called to the marriage supper of the Lamb!'" And he said to me, "These are the true sayings of God."

- Every time we read of praise in the Book of Revelation it is as the sound of many waters and as the sound of mighty thunderings.
- The praise listed above is because of the Marriage Supper of the Lamb.
- The Bride is wearing a white wedding garment which is a symbol of righteousness.

THE ANGEL IS A REDEEMED MAN

19:10 And I fell at his feet to worship him. But he said to me, "See that you do not do that! I am your fellow servant, and of your brethren who have the testimony of Jesus. Worship God! For the testimony of Jesus is the spirit of prophecy."

- In chapter 1 verse 1 it was stated that God the Father gave the Revelation to Jesus Christ and Christ gave it to an angel.
- The angel showed it to John in a vision and told him to write it down.
- In verse 10 above, John knelt to worship the angel and the angel informed him that he was a redeemed man and his brother in Christ.
- He instructed John to worship God.

- Unfortunately John did not learn the lesson because he makes the same mistake again in chapter 22:8-9.

THE SECOND COMING OF CHRIST

19:11 Now I saw heaven opened, and behold, a white horse. And He who sat on him was called Faithful and True, and in righteousness He judges and makes war.

12 His eyes were like a flame of fire, and on His head were many crowns. He had a name written that no one knew except Himself.

13 He was clothed with a robe dipped in blood, and His name is called The Word of God.

14 And the armies in heaven, clothed in fine linen, white and clean, followed Him on white horses.

15 Now out of His mouth goes a sharp sword, that with it He should strike the nations. And He Himself will rule them with a rod of iron. He Himself treads the winepress of the fierceness and wrath of Almighty God.

16 And He has on His robe and on His thigh a name written: KING OF KINGS AND LORD OF LORDS.

- This is the climax of all the judgments recorded in the Book of Revelation.
- Christ returns to earth to claim victory at the Battle of Armageddon.
- The title of this book is *Armageddon Ahead.* Now we are reading the final round of this, the most bloody and most destructive battle of all time.

CHRIST'S COMING TO THE AIR AND TO THE EARTH

Before we conclude the climax of the Battle of Armageddon, let us compare the Rapture when Jesus comes to the air for His saints and the Revelation when He comes to the earth with His saints to fight at the Battle of Armageddon:

- At the Rapture the dead in Christ are resurrected; at the Revelation there is no record of a resurrection.
- At the Rapture Christ comes to complete our salvation; at the Revelation Christ comes to declare war against His enemies.
- The Rapture is called the Day of Christ; the Revelation is called the Day of the Lord.
- The Rapture is called the Coming of Christ; the Revelation is called the Second Coming of Christ.
- At the Rapture the salvation of the church will be complete; at the Revelation, Christ will save the Jews from the hands of the Antichrist.
- At the Rapture Christ will take the saints to heaven; at the Revelation Christ will bring the saints to earth from heaven.
- At the Rapture Christ will judge the church and give them their rewards; at the Revelation Christ will judge the nations.
- At the Rapture the saints of all ages will prepare to be the bride; at the Revelation the bride becomes an army to fight with Christ and the angels at the Battle of Armageddon.
- The Rapture will allow the rise of the Antichrist; at the Revelation the Antichrist will be cast into the Lake of Fire.
- The Rapture takes place before the seven year tribulation; the Revelation takes place at the end of the tribulation.
- At the Rapture God's Kingdom is in heaven; at the Revelation God's Kingdom comes to earth.
- At the Rapture God's throne is in heaven; at the Revelation God rules the nations from His throne on earth.
- At the Rapture Christ comes to the air personally in bodily form; at the Revelation He returns on a white horse with the armies of heaven (the redeemed and the angels).
- At the Rapture He comes to receive the redeemed unto Himself; At the Revelation He comes with a sword in His mouth to destroy His enemies.
- At the Rapture He is called Lord, at the Revelation He is called, Faithful and true; the Word of God; King of Kings and Lord of Lords; and He has a new name.

- At the Rapture there is no description of Him, at the Revelation there is a vivid and a detailed description of Him.
- At the Rapture there is comfort for the faithful; at the Revelation there is judgment for His enemies.
- At the rapture He comes in the clouds. At the revelation He stands on the Mount of Olives.

ARMAGEDDON—THE SUPPER OF THE GREAT GOD

19:17 Then I saw an angel standing in the sun; and he cried with a loud voice, saying to all the birds that fly in the midst of heaven, "Come and gather together for the supper of the great God,

18 that you may eat the flesh of kings, the flesh of captains, the flesh of mighty men, the flesh of horses and of those who sit on them, and the flesh of all people, free and slave, both small and great."

- The Battle of Armageddon is called the Supper of the great God in several Scriptures (Ezekiel 39:4, 17-23; Isaiah 34:3).
- Vultures and flesh eating birds will feed on the flesh of the armies of the Antichrist slain in battle.

ANTICHRIST DESTROYED AT THE BATTLE OF ARMAGEDDON

19:19 And I saw the beast (the Antichrist), the kings of the earth, and their armies, gathered together to make war against Him who sat on the horse and against His army.

20 Then the beast was captured, and with him the false prophet who worked signs in his presence, by which he deceived those who received the mark of the beast and those who worshiped his image. These two were cast alive into the lake of fire burning with brimstone.

202

21 And the rest were killed with the sword which proceeded from the mouth of Him who sat on the horse. And all the birds were filled with their flesh.

- Verse 21 presents an additional statement that the birds ate the flesh of those killed in battle.
- The Antichrist and the False Prophet are the first to be cast alive into the Lake of Fire.
- The armies of the Antichrist will be destroyed by the spoken word of Christ symbolized by the sword out of His mouth.

CHRIST WINS THE VICTORY

- When Jesus returns, the Battle of Armageddon will be the supremacy of the Kingdom of God over the kingdom of Satan.
- On the winning side are:
  Christ.
  The redeemed.
  The angels.
  The sheep nations who ally with Israel against the Antichrist.

CHRIST'S ENEMIES DEFEATED

- On the losing side are:
  The Antichrist.
  The False Prophet.
  The devil, the fallen angels and the demons.
  The goat nations—those nations that have allied with the Antichrist against Israel
- The armies under the command of the Antichrist will be destroyed by a word from the mouth of Christ (chapter19:18-19, 21).
- The judgment of the nations is described in Matthew 25:31-46.

REVELATION:
CHAPTER TWENTY

Finally, Satan is overthrown, the unsaved will face the Great White Throne Judgment, and the Book of Life is opened for the redeemed.

SATAN BOUND FOR 1,000 YEARS

20:1 Then I saw an angel coming down from heaven, having the key to the bottomless pit and a great chain in his hand.
2 He laid hold of the dragon, that serpent of old, who is the Devil and Satan, and bound him for a thousand years;
3 and he cast him into the bottomless pit, and shut him up, and set a seal on him, so that he should deceive the nations no more till the thousand years were finished. But after these things he must be released for a little while.

- The first three verses of chapter 20 are still dealing with the end of the seven year tribulation and the climax of the Battle of Armageddon.
- Chapter 19 closes with the defeat of the Antichrist, the False Prophet and the nations who allied with them.
- After God has dealt with the Antichrist and the False Prophet, He assigns an angel to bind the devil in the bottomless pit for 1,000 years to prevent him from deceiving the nations.
- The words *1,000 years* are found 6 times in this chapter.
- Some teach that the earth will be desolate during the thousand years and the earth will actually be the bottomless pit. There is no Scripture to support this teaching.

- On the other hand the Bible teaches that during the 1,000 year reign of Christ on earth, there will be:
  Universal peace – Isaiah 2:4; 9:6-7.
  Universal prosperity – Isaiah 65:24; Micah 4:4-5.
  Universal Religion. All men will worship Christ the King – Malachi 1:11; Zechariah 13:16-21.
  The Glory of God will be manifest – Isaiah 4:4-6; Ezekiel 43:1-5.
  A new temple – Ezekiel 45:1-5.
  A constant outpouring of the Holy Spirit – Joel 2:28-32; Isaiah 32:5; Ezekiel 36:25-27.
  Universal justice – Isaiah 8:6, 7; 9:6, 7; 11:3-5.
  Life will be extended – Isaiah 65:20; Zechariah 8:4.
  Light will be increased – Isaiah 30:26; 60:18-22.
  Wild animals will be tamed – Isaiah 11:6-8; 65:17-25.
  Harvests will be ripe and productive – Isaiah 65:1-10; 55:12-13.
- Christ and the redeemed will rule the nations.

THE MARTYRED SAINTS REIGN WITH CHRIST

20:4 And I saw thrones, and they sat on them, and judgment was committed to them. Then I saw the souls of those who had been beheaded for their witness to Jesus and for the word of God, who had not worshiped the beast or his image, and had not received his mark on their foreheads or on their hands. And they lived and reigned with Christ for a thousand years.

- The tribulation martyrs have been resurrected and raptured.
- They have a place in reigning with Christ for 1,000 years.
- So far we have read about the resurrection and the Rapture of the saints of all ages. This happened before the seven year tribulation.
- The 144,000 were raptured in the middle of the seven year tribulation.

- The two witnesses were resurrected at the end of the seven year tribulation but there is no record of the resurrection and the rapture of those who were martyred during the entire seen year tribulation until chapter 20 verse 4.
- John saw thrones and judgment was given to the martyrs during the Millennium.
- That means they had been resurrected, raptured and had received their rewards at the Judgment Seat.
- The Bible states that they lived and reigned with Christ 1,000 years.
- Thus they were part of the first resurrection.
- The fact that they lived and were to reign with Christ 1,000 years—verse 4, means that they were resurrected and were part of the Bride at the Marriage Supper of the Lamb.
- They were also part of heaven's victorious army which returned to earth with Christ to defeat the armies of the Antichrist at the Battle of Armageddon.

Two Resurrections

20:5 But the rest of the dead did not live again until the thousand years were finished. This is the first resurrection.
6 Blessed and holy is he who has part in the first resurrection. Over such the second death has no power, but they shall be priests of God and of Christ, and shall reign with Him a thousand years.

- In some ministers' handbooks used for funeral services, it reads, "the general resurrection of the dead."
- Actually, there is no general resurrection of the dead.
- There are two resurrections with 1,000 years between them.
- The first resurrection includes the following:
  The Lord Jesus Christ – the First Fruits.
  Those resurrected and caught up at the Rapture – the Harvest.
  The 144,000, the tribulation martyrs, and the two witnesses – the Gleanings.

- Those who are part of the first resurrection will escape the second death.
- The second death is eternal separation from God in the Lake of Fire (verse 14).

SATAN'S FINAL REBELLION OVERTHROWN

20:7 Now when the thousand years have expired, Satan will be released from his prison

8 and will go out to deceive the nations which are in the four corners of the earth, Gog and Magog, to gather them together to battle, whose number is as the sand of the sea.

9 They went up on the breadth of the earth and surrounded the camp of the saints and the beloved city. And fire came down from God out of heaven and devoured them.

10 The devil, who deceived them, was cast into the lake of fire and brimstone where the beast and the false prophet are. And they will be tormented day and night forever and ever.

- Many have asked, *Why does God release the devil when he has had him imprisoned for 1,000 years?*
- The answer is that God is just.
- The believers will enjoy an eternal and a glorified body like the body of Jesus, but the people over whom we shall reign will have families during the Millennium.
- Among the nations, life will be extended so that if someone dies at 100 years of age, it will be like a child dying (Isaiah 65:20).
- This means that people who are born during the Millennium will never know temptation from a personal devil.
- A just God must allow them to be tempted and tormented by the enemy, even as we are today.
- Mankind must be given a choice.
- It is incredible that after enjoying 1,000 years of peace and prosperity with Jesus reigning personally over the entire

world, when Satan is loosed from the pit, many nations will again be deceived by Satan.
- They will be influenced by the devil to declare war on Jerusalem, the city which is the capital of Christ's Kingdom world wide.
- The Bible declares that Fire will fall from heaven and destroy the rebel nations.
- Satan and all his hosts will be cast into the Lake of Fire and Brimstone where the Beast and the False Prophet are. They were cast into the Lake of Fire when Christ returned to earth to win the Battle of Armageddon.
- The Lake of Fire is eternal hell.

THE GREAT WHITE THRONE JUDGMENT

20:11 Then I saw a great white throne and Him who sat on it, from whose face the earth and the heaven fled away. And there was found no place for them.

12 And I saw the dead, small and great, standing before God, and books were opened. And another book was opened, which is the Book of Life. And the dead were judged according to their works, by the things which were written in the books.

13 The sea gave up the dead who were in it, and Death and Hades delivered up the dead who were in them. And they were judged, each one according to his works.

14 Then Death and Hades were cast into the lake of fire. This is the second death.

15 And anyone not found written in the Book of Life was cast into the lake of fire.

- The Great White Throne Judgment is the judgment for the devil and the unsaved.
- John saw the dead stand before God.
- These are the unsaved dead who were not in the first resurrection.

- The earth and the heaven fled away. This does not mean the cessation of the heavens and the earth.
- It refers to the complete renovation of the universe by fire.

THE BOOK OF LIFE

- The Book of Life is the book that contains the names of the redeemed.
- Some scholars teach that the reason for the unsaved to be judged by their works also, is because there will be degrees of punishment in hell.
- It would be unjust if Hitler and the Antichrist suffer the same hell as a good living, moral, unsaved church member.
- The Bible says, *It will be more tolerable for one city than for another city on the Day of Judgment.*
- To be more tolerable for one must mean it will be less tolerable for another.
- Other scholars believe that the books which will judge the works of the unsaved refer to the books of the Word of God which will judge men in that day.

GOD RESTED ON THE SEVENTH DAY

- God spent six days in creation and on the seventh day He rested.
- From Adam until now has been 6,000 years, or six days prophetically.
- When Jesus returns to earth, He will cease from His plan of redemption and enjoy the seventh day, or the 7,000th year with His Bride.

REVELATION:
CHAPTER TWENTY-ONE

J ohn is given a glimpse of the New Jerusalem, God's eternal home.

A NEW HEAVEN AND A NEW EARTH

21:1 Now I saw a new heaven and a new earth, for the first heaven and the first earth had passed away. Also there was no more sea.

- Many people believe that the world will one day come to an end. Not so!
- The Bible teaches that there will be a new heaven and a new earth but it means that the present heaven and earth will be renovated by fire to remove all the results of sin.
- To illustrate, when a person is saved, the Bible speaks of him as being a new creation. It is the same individual, but the person is new.
- In the same way we will still have the heavens and the earth but the results of sin will have been destroyed.
- All things will become new and righteousness will prevail.
- Although the Bible states that there will be no more sea, the Bible refers to rivers, lakes, and bodies of waters for all eternity (Psalm 72).

THE NEW JERUSALEM

21:2 Then I, John, saw the holy city, New Jerusalem, coming

down out of heaven from God, prepared as a bride adorned for her husband.

3 And I heard a loud voice from heaven saying, "Behold, the tabernacle of God is with men, and He will dwell with them, and they shall be His people. God Himself will be with them and be their God.

- The New Jerusalem has several names, including:
  The Holy City.
  The New Jerusalem.
  The Bride, adorned for her husband.
  The Tabernacle of God.
- The city is called the Holy City because sin will be totally destroyed when God renovates the universe by fire.
- The city is already in heaven but will come down out of heaven from God to the earth.
- It is prepared as a Bride for her husband because it will be the eternal home of Christ and His Bride.
- The Bible states when the New Jerusalem comes from heaven to earth that the Tabernacle of God is with men because this city will be God's dwelling place on earth with man forever.

ETERNAL BLISS

21:4 And God will wipe away every tear from their eyes; there shall be no more death, nor sorrow, nor crying. There shall be no more pain, for the former things have passed away."

5 Then He who sat on the throne said, "Behold, I make all things new." And He said to me, "Write, for these words are true and faithful."

6 And He said to me, "It is done! I am the Alpha and the Omega, the Beginning and the End. I will give of the fountain of the water of life freely to him who thirsts.

7 He who overcomes shall inherit all things, and I will be his God and he shall be My son.

The following eternal blessings are available:
- God will wipe away every tear.
- No more death.
- No sorrow.
- No crying.
- No pain.
- All things made new.
- God's promises are true.
- God is eternal and faithful.
- The water of life will be available.
- We will inherit all things.
- We will be part of God's family.

A Solemn Warning

21:8 But the cowardly, unbelieving, abominable, murderers, sexually immoral, sorcerers, idolaters, and all liars shall have their part in the lake which burns with fire and brimstone, which is the second death."

The Lake of Fire, is promised to the following:
- The cowardly (the fearful).
- The unbelieving.
- The abominable (depraved).
- The murderers.
- The immoral.
- People involved in sorcery (witchcraft).
- Idolaters.
- Liars.

The New Jerusalem, the Bride, the Lamb's Wife

21:9 Then one of the seven angels who had the seven bowls filled with the seven last plagues came to me and talked

with me, saying, "Come, I will show you the bride, the
Lamb's wife."

10 And he carried me away in the Spirit to a great and high
mountain, and showed me the great city, the holy Jerusalem, descending out of heaven from God,

11 having the glory of God. Her light was like a most precious
stone, like a jasper stone, clear as crystal.

12 Also she had a great and high wall with twelve gates, and
twelve angels at the gates, and names written on them,
which are the names of the twelve tribes of the children of
Israel:

13 three gates on the east, three gates on the north, three gates
on the south, and three gates on the west.

14 Now the wall of the city had twelve foundations, and on
them were the names of the twelve apostles of the Lamb.

• The angel tells John that he wants to introduce him to the
Bride, the Lamb's wife and he shows him a city.

• Why? Because the city was to be the eternal home of the Bride
and she is identified by the names of the 12 tribes of Israel
which are written on the 12 gates of the city and the names
of the 12 Apostles which are written on the 12 foundations
of the city.

• In other words, the Bride is made up of saints in the Old
Testament and saints in the New Covenant.

THE GLORY OF THE NEW JERUSALEM

21:15 And he who talked with me had a gold reed to measure
the city, its gates, and its wall.

16 The city is laid out as a square; its length is as great as its
breadth. And he measured the city with the reed: twelve
thousand furlongs. Its length, breadth, and height are equal.

17 Then he measured its wall: one hundred and forty-four
cubits, according to the measure of a man, that is, of an
angel.

18 The construction of its wall was of jasper; and the city was pure gold, like clear glass.

19 The foundations of the wall of the city were adorned with all kinds of precious stones: the first foundation was jasper, the second sapphire, the third chalcedony, the fourth emerald,

20 the fifth sardonyx, the sixth sardius, the seventh chrysolite, the eighth beryl, the ninth topaz, the tenth chrysoprase, the eleventh jacinth, and the twelfth amethyst.

21 The twelve gates were twelve pearls: each individual gate was of one pearl, And the street of the city was pure gold, like transparent glass.

We learn several facts about the city:

- The city and the streets were made of pure gold.
- It came from heaven to earth.
- It was filled with the glory of God.
- Her light was brilliant.
- The city was built within four walls with 12 gates, three gates in each wall and each gate was a pearl with an angel standing at each gate.
- The walls were 300 feet high.
- The city had 12 firm foundations; each foundation was made of very costly precious stones.
- It was 1,500 miles square.

GOD'S ETERNAL HOME

21:22 But I saw no temple in it, for the Lord God Almighty and the Lamb are its temple.

- There will be no need for a temple where man must come to worship because God and His Son will live visibly in the New Jerusalem with man forever as Adam and Eve did before they sinned.
- The Bride of Christ will have glorified bodies, like the body of Jesus.

- They will assist Christ in the administration of His Kingdom.
- The nations which live through the tribulation and the millennium will have bodies like Adam and Eve had before the fall.

NO SUN OR MOON IN THE NEW JERUSALEM

21:23 The city had no need of the sun or of the moon to shine in it, for the glory of God illuminated it. The Lamb is its light.
- The sun and the moon will shine forever, but in the city of the New Jerusalem there will be no moon or sun because the glory of God will illuminate it and the Lamb is its light.

THE CAPITAL OF GOD'S UNIVERSAL KINGDOM ON EARTH

21:24 And the nations of those who are saved shall walk in its light, and the kings of the earth bring their glory and honor into it.
- This refers to the sheep nations of Matthew 25, who survived the tribulation period and allied with the Jews against the Antichrist at the Battle of Armageddon.
- They also accepted Christ as King in the Millennium and were not deceived by Satan when he was loosed from the pit.
- These nations will live on planet earth forever as God originally intended Adam and Eve to live on the earth forever.
- Man will come and worship God and His Son in the New Jerusalem.
- These are the nations over which Christ and His Bride will reign forever.

21:25 Its gates shall not be shut at all by day (there shall be no night there).

- There will always be day and night, but in the New Jerusalem there will be no night and there will be constant activity.

21:26 *And they shall bring the glory and the honor of the nations into it.*
- These nations will be the nations who survived the tribulation, lived in the millennium and refused Satan's deceit.
- They will live on the earth for all eternity and Christ and His saints will rule over them.

12:27 *But there shall by no means enter it anything that defiles, or causes an abomination or a lie, but only those who are written in the Lamb's Book of Life.*
- We must make a distinction between those who make up the Bride and the nations who live on the earth forever.
- Both groups have their names written in the Book of Life.
- God is omniscient.
- He can pre-determine the Bride, those whose names are not written in the Book of Life, those people who will live on the earth forever and those nations which will be deceived by Satan at the end of the millennium.

REVELATION:
CHAPTER TWENTY-TWO

The Book of Revelation concludes with a final warning for the unbeliever and a glorious hope for those who have been washed in the blood of the Lamb.

THE RIVER OF LIFE AND THE TREE OF LIFE

- It is interesting that there are only two chapters in the Bible to tell us of future eternity.
- The rest of the Bible, for the most part, tells us how to live during our time on the earth.
- We have now reached the last chapter of the Book of Revelation and we will have one final and brief glimpse into future eternity.

22:1 And he showed me a pure river of water of life, clear as crystal, proceeding from the throne of God and of the Lamb.

2 In the middle of its street, and on either side of the river, was the tree of life, which bore twelve fruits, each tree yielding its fruit every month. The leaves of the tree were for the healing of the nations.

- From God's throne there is a pure river of water of life.
- On either side of the river was the tree of life with 12 fruits which were produced every month.
- The leaves of the tree of life are for the healing of the nations.
- The redeemed will have bodies like Jesus.

- Our bodies will never need healing; they will never die.
- Just as Adam and Eve had to eat of the tree of life in the Garden of Eden in order to live forever, so the nations which live on the earth for eternity will also have to eat of the tree of life to live forever.

NO MORE CURSE

22:3 And there shall be no more curse, but the throne of God and of the Lamb shall be in it, and His servants shall serve Him.

4 They shall see His face, and His name shall be on their foreheads.

5 There shall be no night there: They need no lamp nor light of the sun, for the Lord God gives them light. And they shall reign forever and ever.

- The curse came on man and on the earth because of Adam's sin (Genesis 23:14-19).
- Through the cross, Christ has redeemed us from the curse of the law (Galatians 3:13); but now as we enter future eternity, the final chapter of the Bible informs us that the curse of Adam's sin is finally and forever removed.
- His servants will serve Him—His servants will include the angels of heaven, the redeemed who make up the Bride and the nations who will live on earth eternally.
- There shall be no night there—this refers to the New Jerusalem.
- Day and night will continue forever but in the holy city there will be neither darkness nor night.

CHRIST IS COMING SOON

22:6 Then he said to me, "These words are faithful and true." And the Lord God of the holy prophets sent His angel to show His servants the things which must shortly take place.

7 "Behold, I am coming quickly! Blessed is he who keeps the words of the prophecy of this book."

- The angel who gave this vision to John is concluding his remarks.
- In chapter 1, the angel told John to write the things that shall shortly come to pass and as he concludes with the same theme, he adds the words of Jesus, *Behold, I am coming quickly.*
- The first chapter of the Book of Revelation began with a promise of blessing to the reader and in the last chapter it also contains the following blessing: *Blessed is he who keeps the words of the prophecy of this book.*

THE ANGEL WAS A REDEEMED MAN

22:8 Now I, John, saw and heard these things. And when I heard and saw, I fell down to worship before the feet of the angel who showed me these things.

9 Then he said to me, "See that you do not do that. For I am your fellow servant, and of your brethren the prophets, and of those who keep the words of this book. Worship God."

10 And he said to me, "Do not seal the words of the prophecy of this book, for the time is at hand.

- In chapter 19 verse 10, John had worshiped the angel as he did in verse 8 above.
- Both times the angel gently rebuked and assured him that he was a fellow servant, "and of your brethren the prophets."
- He commanded John again to worship God.
- The prophet Daniel was commanded to seal up his prophecy until the last days.
- John is commanded not to seal the words of the prophecy of this book, for the time is at hand.
- As we explained in the first verse, the Lord wants the church to understand clearly the Book of Revelation, the Majesty of

Jesus the King, and the events of prophecy that are revealed in the Book of Revelation.

NO SECOND CHANCE

22:11 He who is unjust, let him be unjust still; he who is filthy, let him be filthy still; he who is righteous, let him be righteous still; he who is holy, let him be holy still."
- When Jesus comes, there will be no second chance.
- In whatever spiritual condition we are when Jesus comes that will be our lot for all eternity.
- The unjust will be unjust; the filthy will be filthy; the righteous will be righteous and the holy will be holy.

JESUS' LAST MESSAGE TO THE CHURCH

22:12 "And behold, I am coming quickly, and My reward is with Me, to give to every one according to his work.
13 I am the Alpha and the Omega, the Beginning and the End, the First and the Last."
- You cannot read the Book of Revelation without realizing the sense of urgency.
- Repeatedly you read that we are fast approaching the end of time and Jesus is soon to appear.
- When He comes it will be too late to ask for forgiveness.
- Salvation is God's free gift of grace, but when Jesus comes all believers will stand before the Judgment Seat of Christ and their works will be rewarded.

PROMISES TO THE OBEDIENT

22:14 Blessed are those who do His commandments, that they may have the right to the tree of life, and may enter through the gates into the city.

- No one is saved by works but when love is our motivation we want to serve Christ, obey Him and work for Him.
- Those who are motivated by love will earn the right to the tree of life, and may enter through the gates into the city.

THE FINAL WARNING

22:15 But outside are dogs and sorcerers and sexually immoral and murderers and idolaters, and whoever loves and practices a lie.

In the final verses of the Book of Revelation we have another list of people, who will be lost eternally:

- Dogs—False prophets and people involved in immoral perversion are called dogs (Deuteronomy 23:18; Isaiah 56:10-11).
- Sorcerers—people involved in drugs and the occult.
- Immoral people.
- Murderers.
- Idolaters.
- Liars.
- People who associate with liars.

THE FINAL AUTHENTICITY OF THE BOOK

22:16 "I, Jesus, have sent My angel to testify to you these things in the churches. I am the Root and the Offspring of David, the Bright and Morning Star."
- John concludes his writings by reaffirming that it was Jesus Himself who commissioned him to write the Book of Revelation.

22:17 And the Spirit and the bride say, "Come!" And let him who hears say, "Come!" And let him who thirsts come. Whoever desires, let him take the water of life freely.

• It is the Bride of Christ and the Holy Spirit who call men to repentance and faith.

THE BOOK OF REVELATION IS GOD'S INSPIRED WORD

22:18 For I testify to everyone who hears the words of the prophecy of this book: If anyone adds to these things, God will add to him the plagues that are written in this book;

19 and if anyone takes away from the words of the book of this prophecy, God shall take away his part from the Book of Life, from the holy city, and from the things which are written in this book.

• The Book of Revelation began with a blessing and it concludes with a warning.

• All Scripture is given by the inspiration of the Holy Spirit.

• God used men and women to write the words, but every word written in the Bible is the result of Divine revelation and inspiration.

• This is why God warns that anyone who adds to this book will suffer the plagues that are written in this book and anyone who removes any words from this book will suffer eternal punishment.

• As I write this book, *Armageddon Ahead,* I am also teaching a series on Demonology and Deliverance and I am currently dealing with The Doctrine of Demons.

• It is amazing how much of the teachings of cults and sects do not agree with the Book of Revelation.

• Those who add to or take from the words of the Book of Revelation will be judged by Almighty God in this life and God will remove their names from the book of life.

Jesus Is Coming Quickly

22:20 He who testifies to these things says, "Surely I am coming quickly." Amen. Even so, come, Lord Jesus!
21 The grace of our Lord Jesus Christ be with you all. Amen.
- The first chapter of the Book of Revelation and the final chapter of this book promise that Jesus is coming soon.
- John adds, Amen—So be it. Even so, come, Lord Jesus.

God's Benediction of Grace

After writing about the judgments of the seven year tribulation, the hostility of the Antichrist, and the horrors of the Battle of Armageddon, I will close my book the way John closed his book, *The grace of our Lord Jesus Christ be with you all. Amen.*

FOR A COMPLETE LIST OF
MEDIA RESOURCES OR
TO SCHEDULE THE AUTHOR FOR
SPEAKING ENGAGEMENTS,
CONTACT:

DR. ROY HARTHERN
ROY HARTHERN MINISTRIES, INC.
P.O. BOX 917737
LONGWOOD. FLORIDA 32791

PHONE: 407-699-6925
EMAIL: royharthern@cfl.rr.com
WEBSITE: www.royharthern.org